P9-AGF-303

The Bible, Live

D0790741

The Bible, Live

A Basic Guide for Preachers and Teachers in Small Churches

Dr. Vernal Wilkinson

Outskirts Press, Inc.
Denver, Colorado

The opinions expressed in this manuscript are solely the opinions of the author and do not represent the opinions or thoughts of the publisher. The author has represented and warranted full ownership and/or legal right to publish all the materials in this book.

The Bible, Live
A Basic Guide for Preachers and Teachers in Small Churches
All Rights Reserved.
Copyright © 2011 Dr. Vernal Wilkinson
All Scripture taken from the New American Standard Bible®, Copyright © 1960,1962,1963,1968,1971,1972,19 73,1975,1977,1995 by The Lockman Foundation. Used by permission.
v4.0

This book may not be reproduced, transmitted, or stored in whole or in part by any means, including graphic, electronic, or mechanical without the express written consent of the publisher except in the case of brief quotations embodied in critical articles and reviews.

Outskirts Press, Inc.
http://www.outskirtspress.com

ISBN: 978-1-4327-6639-9

Outskirts Press and the "OP" logo are trademarks belonging to Outskirts Press, Inc.

PRINTED IN THE UNITED STATES OF AMERICA

Acknowledgements.

I would like to acknowledge the blessing and benefit of my wife in the lifetime of preaching I have enjoyed. She has served me as a spiritual audience of one. If I win her approval, I have succeeded in my goal. I thank Village Missions, my co-laborers, mentors and supervisors who have given me so much input. I also thank Diana Savage for her careful editing.

This book is dedicated to Dr. Glenn F. O'Neal. As a teacher of many of us who serve the pulpits of America and elsewhere Glenn taught us to strive for excellence. He taught a simple method that if practiced diligently by his students could provide the basis of clear exposition. That method is at the center of this book. But Glenn also taught us to strive for integrity in the pulpit. Integrity at the core of the preacher's life and ministry goes much further in securing success in the pulpit than any methodology alone.

Table of Contents

INTRODUCTION

"This show has been recorded before a live studio audience." A comment like this has prefaced many TV shows over the years. It meant that the drama or comedy was performed as a whole without cuts or edits before an audience that responded real time to the story. In some ways the small church is the live studio audience. The sermon is acted out not as a performance for a finished product but as an interactive relationship with the audience. That relationship starts before the camera begins to roll.

The small church is a community that knows its members, including the pastor, in the broader setting of life. This relationship with the speaker plays a larger role in the sermon's effectiveness than does any other factor. When the pastor delivers a sermon, it is given in the context of relationship. The audience interacts with the person as well as the content of the sermon.

This book is about teaching a lesson or delivering a sermon in the context of the relationships that uniquely form the small church. It is about maximizing the context of relationships to achieve effective exposition. It is about letting the Bible drive the content of the message as a revelation from God. But in the desire to communicate with authority in a context where authority might harm the network of relationships the preacher often yields authority to the community. Yet I contend that it is possible to retain the authority of the Scriptures while involving the whole congregation in the search for truth.

Truth must predominate while you prepare to preach. Preparation requires discipline to understand and communicate scriptural truth. You will be challenged to prepare to preach God's message by studying carefully and evaluating the results. This book also offers a format for teaching Bible classes as well preaching to the saints gathered in the small church.

This book is not simply about the method of preaching. It is about a method of teaching and preaching in a way that will mine small-church relationships in order to bring effective life change to your hearers. As you read this work I assume that you have practiced more than one method of preaching a sermon. My intent is not to displace those practices. Rather I want to broaden the array of tools at your disposal for sermon preparation by adding a method of preaching that fits a small-church setting.

This book is not about preaching. I assume that you already prepare and deliver expository sermons. It is not about rhetorical theory either. Many other works have been written about that subject.

This book is about how to structure the lesson and the sermon in a way that best matches the characteristics of the small church. You can be assured that with this method, the Scriptures will be expounded faithfully and your sermon can be solidly based on good exegesis without compromise. Yet that exegesis can simply and clearly be made relevant to the small congregation. With this method you can test your lesson or sermon for clarity and use an open ended format that will help draw the audience to own the conclusions of the exposition. You will be able to build on that ownership to help your congregation establish practices that reflect biblical discipleship.

Pastors of small churches come from varying backgrounds. Some have had seminary training. Most have not because small churches cannot pay the salaries that larger churches can. Also, small churches usually are not as attractive to seminary graduates since they are limited demographically or geographically. If you have seminary training and you are in a small church, you are there most likely because of one of two reasons. The first is that your denomination or someone who gave you career direction thought that experience in a small church would be good before you were promoted to a larger work. Second, you've had a successful career pastoring medium to large churches. Now you are retired and use your well honed skills part-time in a small church to supplement your retirement income. If either of these situations apply to you, you may wish to read just parts one, three and four to help you use your skills to the best advantage for preaching and teaching in a small-church setting. Add the tools from this book to your good training and experience to help you be as successful as possible in the small church.

Most of us who serve in small churches arrived as the pastor of a small church through a different route than seminary. Starting as laypeople we studied online courses or attended alternative schools for biblical training. These courses, plus diligent personal study, have given us a good knowledge of the Bible. While we may have had courses in speech or communication, the detailed study of sermon preparation and delivery has been a luxury beyond most pastor's budgets. Your ministry to the small church is either as a missionary or as a second vocation after the career that allows you feed your family.

This book is for you. It provides you with an effective model of preparation that will fit into the demands of a missionary or bi-vocational position. This book also teaches how to present effective lessons and sermons in small-church settings that will increase the persuasiveness of your preaching and teaching ministry.

In summary, this book presents a method of teaching and preaching that is especially effective in the small-church context.

PART 1
Organizing the Sermon

When I began my preaching and teaching ministry in a small rural church, a confusing echo of voices began to fill me. These were the voices of pastors I knew and had heard along with the voices of various teachers of communication and exposition I had studied under. Each was telling me how I ought to do ministry according to the person's own philosophy of ministry and preaching. I had to sort out the voices, come to my own philosophy of ministry before the Lord, and organize my sermons accordingly. How you organize a sermon depends on what you believe concerning the nature of the small church and the nature of preaching. For anyone preaching in a small church this section will help to clarify small-church characteristics as well as clarify the philosophy of preaching that matches those characteristics.

CHAPTER 1
ON THE SMALL CHURCH

I once owned a home in a small coastal town. After I moved away, I returned one Saturday to prepare the house to be sold. I ran into a couple of friends from the church I had attended. I mentioned to them about the work I was doing on the house and why. I left the following morning before church began but I returned for the next Sunday service. The pastor greeted me at the door and congratulated me on the sale of my house. I didn't know that it had sold. In fact, the listing was so new, the sign hadn't even been posted yet. But a friend of someone in the church had heard through the grape vine that it was for sale and they had offered my asking price through their real-estate agent. That web of personal relations is a characteristic of the small church.

Characteristics of the Small Church

In organizing your sermon material, it is important to keep in mind the characteristics of the small church. Most churches have 100 or fewer in average worship attendance.[1] Though small, these churches develop the maximum social capital from the network of relationships that characterize the small church. Small churches have the intense face-to-face communications that are essential in developing personal character and community trust.[2] For this reason, the small church defies the principles of management efficiency that work on a large scale. The small church exhibits inherent differences from the large church for this reason. Many have assumed mistakenly that the small church is simply a large church on a reduced scale. Some have tried to duplicate the pattern of the large church in the small church. The small church resists these efforts because it is more than a potential large church.[3] Preaching, like all other aspects of ministry, must accommodate the characteristics of the small church.

Glenn Daman has identified fifteen characteristics of the small church that the preacher must take into account while preparing his sermons.[4]

1. The small church is relationally driven. Relationships are what draw people to church. The church is a big family. As such it nurtures and facilitates family relationships. Programs and ministries center on relationships and their effectiveness is measured by the effect upon relationships. The preacher's relationships within the small-church family will determine how people receive the sermon. Basing the sermon on other foundations of authority such as scholarship, rhetorical skill, or denominational credentials will not work. The sermon must give deference to the relationship that the preacher has to the church family.

2. The small church works through informal channels. Decisions are not made by formal voting but over coffee around a kitchen table. Life change is more likely to take place in an informal setting than in an altar call or special spiritual emphasis week. Even when those appeals work, they do so because informal channels of communication have sanctioned those kinds of events as proper places to express a change already decided upon. The sermon should be aimed at the individual

not as a seeking soul but as a member of the community of faith.

3. The small church works as a whole unit and not just through the pastor, boards, or committees. The entire congregation makes decisions as a democracy rather than as an ecclesiastical hierarchy. When sermons deal with issues such as polity, mission, evangelism, fellowship, etc., the pastor coaches the whole group to adopt a new ethic in these areas rather than adopt the correct view or a policy as a result of the sermon. This slows the process of change but makes the changes more likely to occur.

4. Power and authority remain with the laity. Many small and especially rural churches have had the pastors come and go over the years. As a result pastors are not regarded as essential to the operation or even the health of the church. While most small churches highly value preaching, they don't require or even expect rhetorical excellence in order to pay attention to the sermon. You cannot expect to be heard, much less heeded, simply because you hold the title or fill the office. However, because preaching is valued, if you are sensitive to the permissive nature of your position, you can structure your sermon accordingly. When you tacitly admit that power and authority lie with the congregation, you seek permission for a hearing based on a common regard for the Word of God.

5. Family relations characterize the small church. The new preacher must be adopted into the family. This will not happen because the sermons are outstanding but rather because significant members of the family give approval and make a place for the new preacher. This adoption process takes time. You learn the vocabulary and values of the church family before you can reflect them in your sermon. You must learn to respect those values and to reinforce the good in the church's

spiritual life before you are accepted. Only then will the people accept your sermons. Therefore, your sermon structure should be simple, straightforward and regular during the adoption period. Later familiarity will allow you greater latitude in organizing your material and delivery.

6. Communication in the small church takes place through a grapevine of connections. Therefore you should attempt to make your sermons the subject of grapevine communication. You know that you have succeeded when reports come back to you that others are discussing the sermon. When the points of the sermon, illustrations, and personal anecdotes get grapevine attention the sermon's effectiveness is enhanced.

7. Tradition and heritage provide the floor for present church ministry. Stories from the past are what the present generation uses to build meaning and value into the church's current ministry and out reach. While these may appear to be entrenched traditions that hinder growth, you must organize your sermon material to allude to, if not fully endorse, these stories. If you will reframe the stories and the understanding of them in biblical terms you can align the church's values with the church's biblical mission. You do this through faithful exposition of the Scriptures illustrated by the stories that contain the church's heritage.

8. In its programs, the small church doesn't separate the generations. With the possible exception of the Sunday school hour, small churches usually don't separate the children from the seniors for worship or other activities. In the same way, structure your sermon to be inclusive. Expand your vocabulary and illustrations to connect with everyone. You should include examples of how to apply the message for those in school settings as well as those in the declining health of old age.

9. In the small church people matter more than perfor-

mance. The person matters more than the program. People are not replaced by those who do a better job. People's performance of a ministry job will be accepted because of who they are in the community. Your sermon will be valued more by how you are accepted than by how good your delivery is. Furthermore, referring in a positive way to people in the congregation during the sermon makes it more effective. When you master these two aspects of the personal nature of the small church, you enhance effective exposition. So, as you grow into a recognized niche in the structure of relationships your sermons become more acceptable.

10. In the small church everyone participates. No matter the age or ability, each individual has an expected assignment. The level of participation is higher because of this value for including everyone. You must also deliver your message with this same sense of inclusiveness. Mentioning people by name and affirming their place in the course of the sermon is important. Expect them to participate in the sermon. Structure your sermon to encourage verbal or visible responses as well as non-verbal or subjective responses. It will be better received.

11. The small church values relatedness. Because of the nature of the small community many of the church members are related by birth. Positions of authority are filled by relatives. If a relative is offended for any reason, then that individual must be won back at any cost. This can restrict full and true fellowship. When you are faithful to preach the Word of God, you have the greatest potential for breaking the power of bloodlines by the call of God's Word.

12. Generalists are of greater value than specialists. You cannot expect to be heard because of your expertise alone. Away from the Sunday morning sermon time, you must demonstrate your willingness to do whatever

is needed. This will go far toward fitting you into a re-spected place in the community. In the course of the sermon, when you demonstrate a passing knowledge of the life and work of your parishioners you will also win the audience.

13. Everyone has a place. An individual's physical pres-ence is attached to a place in the church. Parking spaces and pews have invisible (even sometimes vis-ible) names written on them. If someone's place is not filled, then their absence is noted. Eye-contact is important because the eye-contact of the preacher during the sermon acknowledges the person in his or her place. Through eye contact you form a bond with audience members and validate their attention to the message.

14. The small church's calendar is directly tied to the sea-sons and employment in the area. As we will note later this will impact the planning of your preaching program.

15. Giving is a ready response to an appeal for a need. Small-church people give for a personal need and not for a program. When people in the small church see someone in need they respond and encourage one another to give. When your sermon seeks giving as a response you should make the appeal personal. In addition to money, your appeal to give time, prayer, encouragement, etc., will get a response as long as the need is obvious.

This list of small-church characteristics highlights the fact that the small church is relationship based and the small church is participatory in nature. Keep these two descriptions in mind as you prepare to preach.

Small-Church Characteristics and Preaching

The smaller the church is the more likely that you will be outside of the network of relationships that make up the church family. The smaller the church, the more necessary it is that you approach the task of preaching as a servant to that family. You should not assume that since the church is small and has difficulty finding and keeping a preacher, you are the big fish in the small pond and that the congregation will appreciate your profound orations. This approach to preaching, that assumes higher authority and power, is offensive. A better preparation to preach builds relationships by serving the people away from the pulpit so that you secure a place in the network of relationships before entering the pulpit. When the sermon is presented, you must do so in the spirit that it is offered humbly as nourishment for the family of God.

Exposition best meets the relationship criteria of the small church. First, the source for exposition is the text of the Bible. The message drawn systematically from the Bible is not yours but God's. The expository sermon levels the relationship between you and the congregation. Both are recipients of the message. Your authority is not personal but arises from the text itself. The greater your appeal to the text for authority, the greater the appeal you will have to the small-church congregation. So expository preaching will carry greater weight.

Second, the expository sermon is more preacher-neutral. It matters less how brilliant or insightful you may be. Your performance and the experience of hearing you need not be thrilling. It matters more how faithful you are to the text. Faithfulness is a respected virtue; therefore, faithfulness in the sermon will be respected. Exposition undergirds you with faithfulness and humility as you deliver God's message faithful to its context and relevant to the modern audience.

You must also structure the sermon to invite participation. In your delivery continue to invite the congregation to join in the search for God's message. The expository message that calls for inquiry into the text will cause the small-church congregant to feel invited to participate.

Preaching Program

Keeping the characteristics of participation and relationship in mind, develop the preaching program to meet the needs of the small church congregation.

The small church orients its life more to oral presentation rather than visual. It is common for people to tell and listen to stories of local heritage that include the histories and news of local people. The personal relationship that people have with the pastor during the sermon is one of speaking and listening. Therefore, you should limit the use of PowerPoint or video clips or drama. Instead develop the preaching program as a conversation between you and the members of the small church. A conversational style of delivery that stays away from the trappings of a production will appeal more broadly and be more relevant.

Develop the preaching program as a series of conversations framed around the message of the Bible in a book of the Bible or a biblical biography. Keep in mind that these themes are not random. A properly developed preaching program correlates with the needs of your congregation as you understand them. Compare those needs to theological themes communicated in portions of Scripture. Then study those portions as the basis of subsequent sermons in the series. Exposition has unique value at this point for the small-church congregation. Rather than preaching to the congregation's need or teaching about that need, exposition invites the congregation to discover God's message and apply it to their own context. The expositional sermon becomes an inductive study involving congregational participation.

In developing the preaching program keep in mind the local context. Larger urban and suburban churches identify themselves in the context of the majority culture. Preaching addresses issues common to that majority culture. The small church, however, is more isolated, family-focused and embedded in the local community. Therefore, the preaching program should bring God's message to bear on that context. The Montana wheat farmer is not concerned about the issue of same sex marriage in California. He will be more concerned about enough moisture for his dry-land wheat. So a sermon on same sex marriage will not meet his need for God's message. Somewhat more interesting would be a sermon addressing global warming and its effect on moisture levels. But preaching how one trusts God in a fallen world would grip the farmer when he waits for rain to sprout the wheat because it focuses on the most immediate local context.

Preaching Plan

Plan for the long haul. Someone did a study of farmers and the process of change in farming practices. When a new hybrid seed that promised greater yields was introduced, a few of the study group of farmers tried the seed[5]. After a couple of seasons, a few more influential farmers also tried the seed, and as a result, the majority of farmers in the study group switched to the new seed with just a few holdouts who later adopted the new seed. Similarly, change in the small church takes time. It is incremental. Those who are community leaders or tribal chiefs will influence others by their choices[6]. Plan to preach for slow change over a long term. Look for those who respond, and build on their response to help bring necessary change to the rest of the congregation and even the broader community.

Because one sermon will not make a huge difference all by itself, set forth a sermon plan that fits within the life of the congregation and community. Select the length of the Scripture passage according to the exegesis you can do and the sermon you can prepare in the weekly schedule appropriate to Sunday-by-Sunday preaching. Fit those sermon series into the calendar of events in the church and community life.

The calendar in the small community may be different from that of larger communities. In one resort community, Memorial Day was an important holiday because it was the first long weekend of the summer season. Visitors would increase, so resort operators would start to be less regular in attendance. Beginning a summer series on that weekend allowed that time to be special in the life of the congregation. Another community highlighted soil-conservation Sunday in the annual calendar. Some members of the congregation had received national awards for soil-conservation practices. Planning a series around the doctrines of creation was effective at this time. Blend the local calendar with the Christian calendar in order to efficiently plan your annual preaching program.

Sermon series can be of different types. The most obvious is a series of preaching through a book of the Bible. The book you choose should contain themes addressed to the original audience that are the same ones needed by the contemporary audience. In planning the series, read the book of the Bible and with the help of survey works outline it. Then plan the individual sermons that you will deliver in sermon units. These units should be digestible by you in preparation and by the congregation as you deliver them.

A doctrinal series is most useful in conjunction with the Christian calendar. You could preach the doctrines of the incarnation during Advent or preach the atonement around Lent.

In a biographical series, you can emphasize the Lord's action in and through a biblical character. Each sermon in this series can be a story from the individual's life. Some holidays and special events lend themselves to sermons from passages dealing with compatible topics. Between Mother's Day and Father's Day you could do a series on marriage and family.

You can interrupt the longer series on a book of the Bible to do a shorter seasonal series corresponding to the local or Christian calendar. Break off the longer series at a point where the book being studied naturally shifts its topics or sequence in some way. Then initiate the shorter series. When you return to the longer series, review the development of biblical theology up to that point in the book without taking time to review each of the sermons you preached previously. This will allow you to resume the argument of the book but God's message for God's people will remain the focus of the Sunday sermon.

Sermon Notes for Review

How many small church members does it take to change a light bulb? Just one but first everyone must talk about the change. They must compare it to all the past changes in lighting. Then the patriarch and matriarch of the church must designate someone to change the bulb. Then the person who donates the use of the ladder must agree with the person who gets the bulbs to meet with the person who holds the ladder to be present when the bulb-changer can actually make the exchange.

How does the nature of the small church impact preaching?

1. Through its characteristics of relationships and participation
2. Through its cohesive community plan to preach to its unique context

CHAPTER 2
ON PREACHING

In other occupations the goal is clear. In sports it is the score. In manufacturing it is the product. Yet preachers debate, equivocate and even confound the goal of preaching. When I entered the preaching ministry, I dearly hoped to receive approval. Experience taught me that this was an illusive and unachievable goal. There, however, is an achievable goal for preaching in the small church.

Preaching's Goal

The goal of preaching is life-change. All preaching asks listeners to hear the biblical text (Romans 10:14). Yet even when they hear that text, they cannot do so as just a clinical act. Merely the perceiving sound waves in their auditory canals cannot lead them to believe in the sense that the New Testament means to believe. The sermon must be relevant to the value systems and wills of the hearers. Jesus rebuked His contemporaries' shallow hearing by quoting the words of Isaiah, "You will keep on hearing but will not understand..." (Matthew 13:14). Auditory perception and even cognitive recognition were not enough to effect life change unless the will was engaged positively.

At this point many contemporary teachers of preaching have fallen short in sufficiently defining the goal of preaching as described in the Bible. John A. Broadus said that the goal of preaching was to spread the good tidings of salvation through Christ.[7] He said that explanation, accomplishes the goal of preaching. While his definition is helpful, it doesn't expect anything to happen in the hearer. Haddon W. Robinson goes a step further.[8] He extends the goal of preaching from communication to relevant communication by adding that the preacher must make application to the hearers. Like Broadus, he believes the preacher should explain but must also develop a relationship between the ancient biblical truth and the modern hearer. These two like many others recognize that education is not the goal of preaching. If it were, then the sermon's success could be measured by quizzing on the sermon's content. These authors do not go far enough.

Glenn O'Neal's definition of the goal of preaching is, "… to communicate the revelation of God, contained in the Word of God and to relate it to the needs of people."[9] O'Neal is on the right track. The sermon's application must be based on the needs of people. The preacher must not communicate only the Word of God but also communicate that Word to the known needs in the hearers. This goal bridges the gap between the Bible and the audience better than the simple explanation of Broadus or even the modern terminology or accommodation of interest that Robinson promotes. O'Neal says that preaching should identify the need of people and point the people to find the fulfillment of their needs in the biblical text. But that stops short of the true goal of preaching. The audience senses the relevance but remains passive to the message's expectation. Neither Jesus nor Paul wanted hearers who understood but remained passive. They wanted listeners to turn (Matthew 13:15) and believe (Romans 10:14).

The goal of the sermon must be life change. Dr. Lori Carrell reported that the majority of preachers she surveyed made *change* the goal of every sermon.[10] This is the correct ultimate goal, but it is not achieved solely on the efforts and performance of the preacher. The work of the Holy Spirit through the inspired Word of God is what brings about change. However, we preachers must do our part in the development, structure and delivery of sermons. We must strive to see God work change in the lives of our parishioners through the power of preaching. Most preachers, either explicitly or implicitly, make change their goal when they preach. Life-change may take place through knowledge, actions, choices, words, values, beliefs, perceptions, or attitudes. But the change we seek at the end of preaching is not limited. It is as varied as both the Bible itself and the creative enterprise of the Holy Spirit. However, the goal of preaching remains life change.

When we set out to prepare and deliver sermons, we prepare to change lives. Though educating about the Bible is a worthwhile goal for a class lesson, it is not enough to constitute the proper end of preaching (See part 3). The sermon should make the Bible relevant to the audience members so that understanding of the text is expanded. When you exegete not only the text but also the needs of the audience and bring the two together, you may point to the Scripture as the potential source for fulfilling those needs. However, this needs-based approach still leaves the outcome up to the hearer. You must structure preaching to build in an expectation for life-change in your audience.

Because of the integrated nature of the small church, life-change is the most appropriate goal. Single-focused sermons fail to take into account how the church family influences the process of development. When you preach sermons for cathartic experience, for education, for organizational goals, or for therapeutic help, you shortsightedly ignore the spiritual formation that takes place through informal decisions made with the counsel of the body and your direction as pastor. By adopting the broader goal of life-change, you will make a much more significant impact on the lives of your people.

Sermon Types

Different types of biblically based sermons are usually cat-alogued as *textual, topical* and *expositional*.[11] Each of these makes the Bible the starting point for the developing the ser-mon. However, each treats that beginning point differently.

The textual sermon begins with a concept from a Bible text. That becomes the only biblical point of reference for the remainder of the sermon. You develop the concept not from the text itself but from your own research and ingenuity. You use other sources to analyze, explain, and illustrate the concept. Any appeal you make to the audience to change or take action is based on the logic or urgency that you have developed. The weakness of this approach is that the text is merely a springboard to develop a thought. The text suggests the thought, but it is not tied to the broader message of God in the biblical context. The authority for the message comes from you or the sources you use to develop the message. The small church resists this kind of authority. If you exegete the text and its context, then the points or the ideas you get from it could be consistent with the text but not necessarily derived from it. That makes the textual sermon good devotional message. However, a steady diet of men's thoughts, however moving, will not bring the potential for life-change that the Word of God promises. A textual sermon then is taken from a thought suggested by a biblical text but developed by your own reflec-tions, logic and resources.

The topical sermon provides information from the Bible that you have collected on a given topic. You determine the topic and the texts to be used. Then you study all the relevant texts to understand what the Bible has to say about the topic. The points are a collection of texts from different parts of the Bible that ostensibly deal with this topic. However, the topical sermon does not carry the power of God's message to His people. It can treat the Bible as an encyclopedia of knowl-edge or a self-help book consisting of God's suggestions for a better life. The topical sermon is liable to use a biblical text to explain a topic that it does not, in fact, address. For example, the topic of receiving salvation has been incorrectly drawn from Revelation 3:20 when the context shows that the passage is actually directed to believers. When paired with good exegesis a topical study can provide a good summary of important truths but not a sermon. Systematic theologies are built from collections of verses on the various theological categories. A topical sermon is based on a collection of texts that deal with a topic.

Communicating biblical truth through exposition has been much maligned and much misunderstood. Expositional preaching seeks to expose what the Bible has to say in its context to the modern audience.[12] Some think that exposition was just a reading of the text. But it does more for it aims to uncover the text's message. Some people assume that simply covering the sequence of the verses in a long text constitutes exposition. However, while exposition does deal with scriptural texts, long or short, it seeks to uncover the message that the original hearers would have understood in the context in which it was delivered. In so doing today's hearers can better grasp God's message. Exposition goes even deeper than that. It helps us understand the biblical theology of the passage. So exposition results in bringing God's message as understood by the original hearers with its consequent theology into a context that the modern audience can understand. God's message from the scripture as effectively applied by the Holy Spirit (John 17:17) effects life-change. That's the goal of preaching. Exposition is the most faithful to the text and most clearly presents the message of God. Therefore, it is the best of the biblically based forms of preaching for bringing about life-change.

In recent years other forms of preaching have been put forward as biblically based. Most common of these are doctrinal preaching and narrative preaching.

Doctrinal preaching can either be telling what a collection of biblical texts has to say about a given doctrine, or explaining what each text says about one or more theological doctrines. Timothy George says, "Every doctrinal sermon must be contextually rooted in sound exegesis; and every expository or biblical sermon should place a given passage in the widest theological framework possible."[13] In other words both understandings of doctrinal preaching fit other categories. When you summarize what Bible texts have to say about a doctrine, it really is a form of topical preaching. If you do the exegesis well, then you can construct an understanding from the texts that teach the doctrine. Also, in every expositional message you present, you must bring out the text's biblical theology and how the doctrine fits into the broader understanding of progressive revelation. Viewed in this way doctrinal preaching can fit into the categories of topical and expositional preaching.

Narrative preaching likewise fits with the above categories. Narrative preaching can mean simply preaching consistently with the narrative texts of the Bible. H. Grady Davis pointed out some time ago that nine tenths of the Bible is narrative.[14] When the text is telling a story, the good expositor will preach story and not propositions. In this sense narrative preaching is good expositional preaching because the story is the message. One example is when you tell a story to bring home a moral lesson to the hearer. The weakness of this approach is that it detracts from the authority of God in the Bible and places that authority on the storyteller. It also leaves the listener only at the point of insight. Without a call or expectation to act the listener is a passive arbiter of any life-change. You can use extended stories with expositional messages as more than anecdotal illustrations. You can tell a story about "John Everyman" in your sermon's introduction. As you expound the text you pick up the story of "John Everyman" and recount his experience in light of the text. Conclude your message by telling about John Everyman's success or failure in applying the text and the consequences he reaped. Narrative can be a tool of faithful exposition but not a substitute for it.

So, when these three types of biblical preaching - textual,

topical and expositional - are based upon good exegesis they can be effective. But exposition is the preferred form of preaching because it is faithful to the biblical text and is conducive to life-change. Develop material from the Bible through good exegesis of the text and organize it to expose what the Bible has to say in its context to the modern audience. Expositional preaching will be the emphasis for the remainder of this book.

Not all preachers embrace exposition of the Word in the small church. They fear that this more traditional form of preaching doesn't fit small-church characteristics — relationship and participation. David Ray has suggested congregation-based preaching where the preacher lets the congregation spontaneously form the message's conclusion or the preacher simply reads the Scripture and lets them comment. Another version is Chinese Fortune Cookie Sunday where the congregation is given slips of paper with thoughts written on them, and each person is asked to comment during the sermon time.[15] Others have tried a dialogue approach where the preacher reads a passage and then asks a series of questions that the congregation responds to.[16] These approaches compromise the authority of the Word of God and elevate the congregation's authority. Exposition has the advantage of raising the respect the congregation feels toward the pastor while moving the pastor out of the position of authority. That allows the authority of God's Word to stand paramount. For the small church, Glenn Daman emphasizes the need for exegetical preaching that exposes the text's biblical theology: "...every sermon and every principle drawn and applied should be theologically based."[17]

Elements of a Sermon

The elements of the sermon, *logos*, *ethos* and *pathos* are not pieces of the sermon structure such as the introduction, body and conclusion. Rather, these Aristotelian elements describe the whole listener/speaker communication we call a sermon. The *logos* is the sermon's content. When a sermon is expositional, its content comes from the text of the Bible. At its heart is the message to God's people that the text contains. The *ethos* refers to the preacher's character and example. You must be credible. Your credibility comes from your reputation, your self-revelation in the course of preaching and your scholarship or knowledge about the text. All of these combine to create an *ethos* for the speaker. The *pathos* is the audience's emotional and volitional involvement in what you are saying. These elements will be, to varying degrees, necessary in every sermon.

You control these elements. The content or *logos* of your message results from your research and is organized by you either wisely or poorly. You also bring your own reputation or *ethos* to the message. You make yourself known to your audience by your stories, demeanor and manner both inside and outside of the church. Your *ethos* as a small-church preacher is built on your faithfulness to the Word and to your congregation. You also know your audience. It is your responsibility to sway their will and feelings or *pathos* by your preaching. You must attempt to control and manage these three sermon elements to accomplish the objective of each sermon. If your objective is to educate, then the *logos* will take precedence. If your objective is to convict, then *pathos* will take more effort and time. If your objective is to win, then good *ethos* will be paramount to your end.

All three take place simultaneously in the course of delivering a sermon. You must develop *pathos* from the beginning of the message for it to be effective in swaying your audience to life-change at the end of the sermon. To earn a hearing good *ethos* must be apparent at the beginning of the sermon, but it is no less important when authoritatively driving home a point in the sermon's body or in its conclusion. You must weave all three elements together throughout the message to effectively communicate. Everything in your sermon will serve one or more of these parts - *logos*, *ethos* or *pathos*. Consider each act in proclaiming God's Word for how effective it is in developing one or more of these elements. You also need balance. Give some time and consideration to all of these elements at some point in every sermon.

Once in a funeral message I planned to included a word picture about myself when introducing the text. Since I had been the church's pastor ten years earlier and many family members were present whom I did not know, I planned to introduce myself through a word picture of when I'd been in a humorous circumstance. My purpose was to build an *ethos* for myself that was friendly and normal. However, the memories shared about the deceased just before I spoke built the *ethos* of the deceased to the point that I dropped my word picture and built my *ethos* for the message entirely on the reputation of the deceased and my connection with him. Thus my own *ethos* became subservient to that of the person being memorialized. Assuming this position built my *ethos* as a speaker and won a hearing for the subsequent *logos* or content of the funeral sermon because people saw my willingness to defer to the reputation and honor of the one they came to memorialize.

In a small church your *ethos* is paramount to winning the congregation. You will build your *ethos* outside the pulpit in your relationships with people. You will also build a credible relationship with your audience by your openness and faithfulness in the pulpit. As I mentioned before the small church is a family, and the pastor who has a good *ethos* is a respected member of the family. The small-church family respects the virtue faithfulness. When you demonstrate faithfulness outside of the worship context as well as faithfulness to the Bible in the pulpit, you will build a strong *ethos*.

Sermon Notes for Review

"A preacher must - Get in high cotton, put on the wade in the clover, walk about Zion, walk the log, eat high off the hog, ring the changes, shell the corn down in the trough, get on shouting ground, get in a weaving way."[18] But you cannot achieve this kind of effectiveness unless you first organize to preach.

What are essential principles for organizing a sermon for a small church?

1. The goal of life-change should direct the sermon
2. The best type of sermon for the small church is expository
3. Build the sermon on *ethos*

SUMMARY

The characteristics of the small church and the nature of preaching form the basis for organizing of the preaching program of a small church. The sermon should be organized according to the proper goal, the best type, and the most important part. The goal of preaching is life-change. The best of the three sermon types is expository because the small church recognizes the Bible's authority, and the expository sermon appeals to that value. Both the preacher and the congregation submit to the authority of God's Word, and build on the relationship that characterizes the small church. Of the three parts of a sermon - *logos, pathos and ethos* - *ethos* is the most valuable foundation for preaching in the small church. It increases the preacher's capability to relate to the small-church community.

PART 2
Gathering Material

When a man applied for ordination, he was asked, "Do you know the Bible?" He replied, "Yes." Then he was asked what part of the New Testament he knew best. "The story of the Good Samaritan," he said. Instructed to tell the story he said, "There was a good Samaritan going down from Jerusalem to Jericho, and he fell among thorns, and they sprang up and choked him and left him half dead. And he said, 'I will arise.' And he arose and came to a tree, and he got himself hung up in the limb of the tree, and he hung there forty days and forty nights, and the ravens fed him. Delilah, she came along with a pair of shears and cut off his hair and he fell on stony ground. He said, 'I will arise.' He arose and came to a wall, and Jezebel was sitting on the wall, and she mocked him - and he said - 'Chunk her down again.' and they chunked her down again, he said, 'Chunk her down seventy times great, and great was the fall thereof, and of the fragments that remained, they picked up twelve baskets full, and whose wife will she be in the resurrection?"[19]

From classes in Bible college or seminary each preacher has a Bible background - but hopefully a better understanding of its content than the ordination candidate had. The Bible knowledge you have helps you decide what passage you'll preach from or that you'll use to develop a series of messages. However, it is not enough to rely on past education. If you do not have a system of study that allows you to study thoroughly and prepare a sermon Sunday by Sunday, then these chapters will give you ideas and a method to make your study both thorough and reliable for preaching.

CHAPTER 3
STUDY

The preacher to the small congregation, the same as everyone else, must encounter the text afresh. The Bible must have its effect on you through personal devotion as well as careful exegesis. Your *ethos* begins with the integrity of your commitment to the Word of God. If God's Word transforms the life of the preacher, this evidence of the transforming power of the Word of God will build confidence in your audience. In the intense face-to-face relationships that make up every small church the congregation will observe the spiritual force of the Word of God in your personal life.

Steve Bierly warns, "All things tend toward entropy and small church pastors are no exceptions."[20] To counter this, it is essential that you gather material that is new and alive to you.

Encountering the Text

When you prepare a sermon, first read the text in your own language to encounter it afresh. Use a reliable translation to begin to lodge the words of the text in your mind. Then you may branch out to other translations and various paraphrases.

When preparing a series, it is best to read the entire book where each text that you will preach is located. Read through the book more than once at one sitting for the complete effect to register. G. Campbell Morgan is reported to have read a text fifty times before beginning his sermon preparation.

Read introduction material about the text from various sources so you can learn background information and highlight the arguments of the book of the Bible. These sources also give an outline of the biblical book's content so you can compare it to your own planned outline for future sermons. Introduction books often give a heads-up concerning problem texts and offer likely answers to those problems. The best texts for introduction material are Old Testament and New Testament survey-course textbooks. Also the introductory material in commentaries has much to offer. Supplement these materials by researching biblical archaeology and other historical and cultural backgrounds. Notes you make of this introduction material will guide your whole series of sermons and be a great resource for explaining individual Bible passages.

From your reading outline the text for the series. This is an outline of the book for the exegesis you will apply to future sermons. The outline is not for a sermon series. Instead it presents some logical order for the book of the Bible according to the type of literature and the author's purposes. If the book is a didactic section, such as a New Testament letter, then the main points of the argument should be the main points of the outline. For example, most of Paul's letters can be broken into two main points. The first is theological, and the second is practical. However, it is not enough to simply have a two point outline. The outline must develop the author's argument to his contemporary hearers about the issues at hand. In his letter to the Galatians, Paul writes four chapters to solidify his theology and authority against the Judaizers. In the last two chapters he gives practical application for the church. Therefore, an outline of Galatians should have the points of theology in the first four chapters under one heading and the applications of the last two chapters under the second heading.

If the book is narrative, then the sequence of events should dominate the outline. For example, Jonah can be outlined as Jonah in the boat, 1:1 – 17; Jonah under the sea, 2:1 – 10; Jonah in Nineveh, 3:1 – 10; Jonah under the bush, 4:1 – 11. Movements in the story within each chapter become sub-points of the outline.

Books of pure poetry, such as Psalms or Proverbs, defy easy outlining since they don't break down into easily identifiable units. At this point the help of a Bible handbook or a good Old Testament introduction text can provide useful insights. For example, there are at least three different views about the content of the Song of Solomon. The first is allegorical, the second is the love song between Solomon and his bride, and the third is the song of the bride and her true love seeking to escape before Solomon forces her into his harem. Study the theories and make your own decision before outlining the Song of Solomon. Then your outline will reflect the book's development according to that theory. Compare your outline with those of published scholars to determine its accuracy.

Once you've outlined the book's content you can break up the series of messages into the preaching calendar. Each unit of thought in the outline can be the focus of a Sunday sermon. For example the first two chapters of Galatians are about the authority and veracity of the Gospel versus the false gospel brought by false teachers. I preached this as four sermons: "Where is the heart of the Christian firmly rooted?" (1:1 – 5); "How to detect a contrary Gospel?" (1:6 – 10); "What does Paul's biography teach us about the growth of the faith?" (1:11 – 2:10); and "How is what Peter and Paul faced in Antioch like what you and I face today?" (2:11 – 21). Outlining the content of the book is how you plan the sermon series.

Another example would be Jonah. Using the content outline of Jonah I mentioned above, I prepared a series with six sermons. The first sermon, "What would life without God be like?" (1:1 – 4) set the scene for the rest of the story and introduced the series. The second sermon, "How does Jonah demonstrate our conflicts with God?" (1:1 – 17), used Jonah's example to contrast God's work and our attitudes. The third sermon, "How can you and I face desperation with calmness?" (2:1 – 10) focused on Jonah's song of prayer to the Lord when he sank under the sea. The fourth sermon, "What lessons on repentance can we learn from Jonah?" (3:1 – 10), brought out the example of Jonah's repentance and its results. The fifth sermon, "How can Jonah and you and I forgive?" (4:1 – 11), contrasted Jonah's failure to forgive with the forgiving attitudes God wants us to have. The sixth and final sermon in the series covered all the chapters. "How does God communicate with us?" (1:1 – 4:11) focused on God as a communicator with his people and what pattern we can expect.

Before outlining the text for a specific sermon you must read the text and its context. Glenn O'Neal says, "The first task of the expositor is to determine the meaning."[21] The reading of the text from a reliable translation in English or one's native language is the basis for subsequent study. Again O'Neal urges, "Read and reread the passage to be certain you are interpreting it as the writer or speaker intended."[22] Good reading will allow you to establish an outline for your study as a guide. That way you won't study the text as a collection of bits of data instead of a whole communication. Outline the text for the sermon as a content outline.

Study the Text

You should do several types of study concurrently to deepen your understanding of the text. Studying the words of the text is important so you can understand the general denotation before you establish a contextual connotation of the text's important words. Also study the passage's syntax and grammar so you can grasp the nuances of thought that the author communicated to the original audience. The type of literature and the kinds of literary devices used must also be studied. To accomplish all these facets of study, make sure you have the proper resources. O'Neal points out, "The first task of the expositor is to determine the meaning. To do this he needs certain tools, such as, several versions of the Bible, a concordance, a Bible dictionary, and commentaries including critical commentaries..."[23]

Language studies can be very helpful, as well. If you have the skill to handle the Bible's original languages accurately then by all means use that skill to its fullest. This allows you to enter more intimately into the author's mind set and world view. The understanding you gain from the etymology of the original words and the original syntax, allows you to build a better bridge between the ancient and modern worlds. This enhances your exposition and the application of a message to your contemporary audience. However, if you don't know the original languages, you may have confidence in the many English Bible study tools we have today. In fact O'Neal properly exhorts those who may use original languages,

> "A few words of caution are in order for those who handle the original language. Do not give the impression that one cannot really understand the Bible unless he knows the Hebrew or Greek. This is not true and statements or implications to this effect can discourage the listener. Show how the original deepens and clarifies the meaning, but it is unnecessary to declare, 'Now if you knew the original...' It is far better to say, 'This word could be translated...' or 'In another version the word was translated...' ...An interesting thought from the Greek or Hebrew is meaningless unless it contributes to the problem of the message."[24]

Words are the basic units of language. In any language, a word does not have a just one definition. Study carefully to determine which meaning is used in the passage under consideration. One unabridged dictionary gives nine definitions for the word, *the*. The same holds true for the words in the Bible originally written in Hebrew, Aramaic, and Greek. Careful study of the words in that context and similar contexts can help you choose the best definition - the denotation of a word. But the word also has a connotation. You learn this by reading the word with the author's inflection and emphasis. In English there are over fifty ways to say the word, *Oh*[25] The same is true with words in biblical languages. Commentators give insight concerning these nuances. They compare each word with the statements of lexicographers about the word's use in a particular occurrence in order to understand the author's intended connotation. Not every word in the text carries so much weight that it requires such in-depth study. But repeated words certainly do. Varying forms of repeated words define the denotation as well as the connotation that the author intended. For example it would be a mistake to over look *comfort* in 2 Corinthians 1:3 – 4. It is repeated five times in varying forms. Note repeated words and words that are key in the subject and predicate. Commentators will note other significant words that you can add to the list to study in depth.

Sometimes seemingly inconsequential words may turn out to have significance. For example, when Mary and Joseph searched for the young Jesus who had been left behind during the festival, they found Him in the temple. He said to them, "Did you not know that I *had* to be in *My* Father's House?" (Luke 2:49) The italicized words reveal much about Christology.[26] The word, *my* shows us Jesus' understanding, early in His life, of His relationship to God the Father. Because this word implies something about His relationship to Joseph, it also implies knowledge of His true origins. A. T. Robertson has insightful comments about the connotation of *my* in this verse.[27]

A sermon based on a collection of word studies is nothing more than a dictionary. It still fails to communicate the meaning that the author is trying to convey. Syntax, the relationship between words, conveys the meaning between words. In any writing some words represent substantive things while other words move those things into action and relation with other things. Other words remain in a relative position to the main words of the sentence. These words or clauses qualify the main words of the sentence. If you diagramed sentences in school, you understand this relationship. Understanding the subject and predicate of a sentence is essential to understanding the passage's main points. If you can understand these two parts of a sentence in the original language, then you'll understand the meaning. However, even with good, literal, English translations looking at each English sentence for the subject and predicate will help you understand the meaning of the text. Then determine what relative clauses qualify the meaning. These clauses may give time frames, establish geographic connections, or other information. You may even discover the author's purpose or thought.

The same is true for paragraphs. In any language each paragraph is made up of a main point and is usually connected to the topic sentence. The sentences that follow expand, illustrate, qualify, or relate to the main point. You can also diagram the paragraph successfully. Walter Kaiser in *Toward an Exegetical Theology* (see his examples on pages 165 and following) has laid out a fairly simple way to diagram sentences and paragraphs using an English Bible translation. With this method you can identify the main idea of the syntax of sentences and paragraphs to arrive at the meaning of the passage. He uses a variation of this method to treat the stanzas of Hebrew poetry as paragraphs of narrative or didactic prose. The following is an example of how a significant paragraph, such as Romans 12: 1 – 2 may be diagramed. Use a pencil to draw the lines in the following diagram that connect the primary phrases with the words and phrases that describe them.

I urge you

by the mercies of God

brethren

to present your body

a ...sacrifice

living, holy acceptable

to God
spiritual service

and do not be conformed

to this world

but be transformed

by renewing
that you may prove the will of God

good acceptable, perfect

When you use some form of diagramming, you can ensure that the main point of the passage you study will be the main point of the sermon you preach. Even if the form of diagramming you use reminds you of a fourth-grade language text, you will bring the author's intended meaning faithfully to the audience. Another example is Luke 2:49. Considering a syntactical point on the word *had* will help you understand the author's meaning. *Had* sheds light on the filial piety that the Son of God exhibited toward his heavenly Father even at this early stage in his early life. He also reveals that at only twelve years old, he possessed a sense of purpose. Commentaries and lexicons explore these meanings.[28]

You should study the text as literature. The discipline of hermeneutics requires that you stay within the text's literary form when you exegete the passage. When ignoring literary form, a common mistake is to impose didactic meaning on poetic language. This happens often in Proverbs. As wisdom literature, Proverbs is composed of wise sayings in axiomatic statements. The book does not give rules of conduct. Too many sermons have been preached on Proverbs as though they contained a set of rules to live by.

Differing literary genres have differing literary devices. You should identify the literary genre of the text, and analyze the attendant devices. In biblical narrative determine what type of story is being told, such as comedy or tragedy, a quest story or a hero story. Note the motifs and typologies. Uncover the story's plot. In didactic sections, varying arguments are developed. Ask questions such as, "Is this literature primarily written or rhetorical? If the latter, is the argument deliberative as if it were proving a point, epideictic as if it were praising or condemning or forensic as if it were solving a problem?[29]" Much has been written about how the Greek language develops thought versus the way that Hebrew language develops thought, including its chiastic nature. When you pay attention to these literary concerns you will be free from your own cultural biases and will understand the passage much better.

Use of Commentaries

Commentaries contain the information we've just talked about. The commentator lists information about the text, brings together the syntax, significant word meanings, paragraph structure, geography, archaeology, history and literary considerations to help in your understanding. Commentaries discuss the biblical theology of the passage as well. If there are problems or scholars disagree concerning an interpretation, then the commentator will review the significant differences and recommend solutions. Most pastors of local churches don't have the time or resources to investigate thoroughly all the exegetical considerations, review those resources, and blend their individual contributions to the understanding of the text. Commentaries provide a digest of these resources and arrange them in a way that helps you think through the text as you prepare for the sermon. It is important therefore that the commentaries uphold an orthodox view of the inspiration of Scripture.

Commentaries fall into four groupings: devotional, critical, old and new. *Devotional* commentaries look at the personal meaning of the text as applied to the life of the individual believer. They major more on drama and the passage's emotional impact. Such commentaries supplement the *pathos* of the message. *Critical* commentaries dissect the passage and focus on technical aspects of the text from etymology to grammar to culture. They contribute to the *logos* of the message. It takes both kinds: devotional and critical. O'Neal exhorted his students to include critical commentaries in their libraries for study.[30]

Newer commentaries offer recent archaeological and historical discoveries. They also provide more recent cultural information and broadened language understandings. *Older* commentaries are very good at word meanings and syntax and also excel in presenting the passage's biblical theology. Both old and new commentaries are valuable. While the cultural and personal relevance that the newer commentaries offer is valuable, the biblical theology offered by older commentaries applies in any age or culture. Since the small church may be isolated in a rural area or ghetto or ethnic neighborhood it is usually not part of the mainstream of Western culture and small-church pastors will benefit from the biblical theology of the text found in these older commentaries.

After you've done the language study, specifically looking up the words to determine important meanings, I recommend that you turn to commentaries to continue your study. Have about four commentaries handy. Include volumes from a set of Bible commentaries as well as a single-volume commentary devoted to the book you are studying. In these commentaries that you have collected, make sure that one is newer along with one that was produced by a Protestant divine of the past.

Remember that commentaries are not the end and sum of the study of your exegesis. The introduction material along with historical and archaeological information as well as atlases and other sources help set the foundation for your study. Of course any translating you do along with defining key words will precede your use of commentaries. You'll also include diagramming and outlining the passage. There is no substitute for the reading, praying, reflecting, contemplating and meditating on the passage to be preached. All these will give you a variety of insights. Some commentaries will confirm and enhance your insights. You'll throw others out. Along with your insights will come questions that will whet your appetite for the answers and insights you'll find in commentaries.

Sermon Notes for Review

As the new pastor of a small church, I found the task of sermon preparation to be very time consuming. Preparing each Sunday's sermon was the equivalent of writing a major research paper in seminary. Then I realized that the sermon served the Lord among His people and not a grade-point average. To be effective I had to give time to being with God's people. Developing a routine for the studying the text including reading, grammar study, and notes prepared me for structuring a sermon but it also helped preserve time to spend in pastoral duties for the small congregation I served.

What practices of study prepare for the construction of a sermon?

1. The practice of reading
2. The practice of grammatical study
3. The survey of commentaries

CHAPTER 4
FROM STUDY TO THEME

There are four steps for developing your sermon:
1. Read the text of the book or passage to grasp the context of language for the whole sermon process,
2. Study the passage's geographical, social, cultural and historical backgrounds,
3. Analyze grammar, definitions, literary information, and parallel passages in the text,
4. Record all of the above in a set of notes.[31]

Making Notes

O'Neal urged us to make notes of all our work, "Again remember that recording the ideas as you discover them is essential if you want to retain them."[32] When you format your study notes they'll serve you in preparing the sermon at hand as well as for studies in years to come. The best way to format these study notes is according to language and other notations. Break these down into word studies, syntax, and notes. Syntax or language notes should include the diagrams of sentences and paragraphs that have been done. Other notes should include any observations on culture, geography, history, theology, insights, possible applications, etc.

When researching with a Bible software program, you can keep two windows open for documents. Identify each document with the chapter and verse reference followed by "Language" or "Notes." When researching commentaries and other sources from Bible software or when reading the works in a hard-copy volume, type your observations under the individual verse number. When you come across a helpful comment about a word in the text, type your summary of that information under the verse number in the screen document entitled "Language." Do the same with observations on history, biblical theology, or problems/solutions for a verse under that verse number on the document page, "Notes." While you can copy directly from Bible software programs to your own document, I discourage the practice as a usual way of making notes. The process of summarizing in your own words helps you internalize the information. That will assist you in developing insights as you prepare the sermon. When notes are written and formatted in a retrievable way, you will internalize the information about the text. This internalization enhances your integrity in the small church. Your *ethos* is more effective because you have been affected by the text yourself. Your passion for the vitality of God's Word will grow as you experience the value of study. This internalization process leads to more personal notes and observations. As you yourself are impacted by the text's message you become a living example of how applicable the Scripture is in today's context. Recording your careful study and storing it in a system of notes is of great value.

When you have digested a large volume of information regarding a Scripture text in order to grasp its whole meaning, it can be difficult to formulate a complete understanding of the truth from all the bits and pieces you have collected. To overcome this difficulty you may wish to try a conflation of all that information by weaving all the information together into one reading. This reading may be either written or oral. To make an oral conflation, place your notes in front of you. Then begin to read, but amplify the text with additional information from your notes. This would be the same as writing the text out with parenthetical comments interspersed among the words. For example, the line from Luke 2:49 quoted above could be conflated to read, "Did you not know that I *had* (the necessity of His purpose drove Him even at twelve to this place) to be in (aware of his own origins both divine and human) *my* Father's house?" Such a conflation may bring all the details into clear focus.

The next step in sermon construction is moving from raw data to the larger picture.

The Whiting Method

H. Wayne House and Daniel G. Garland credit Arthur B. Whiting for developing a clear system for taking the raw material of exegesis, creating a homiletic outline of the text, and developing an expository message. The Whiting method simplifies an often difficult process. When writing sermons, I have struggled to make the connections necessary to give the biblical text a voice of its own. It is easy to be distracted by current issues, to allow the presentation to become simplistic, or to so overwhelm the audience with the complexities of the text that they lose the message. The Whiting method summarized here gives a firm set of steps that will lead you to clear exposition of the text.

The goal of the following steps is to help you move from the raw data to the principles the passage teaches, to a summary of the passage's theme. The rationale behind the steps is that we can glean, digest and convey in the Sunday-morning sermon the outstanding and abiding principles of God's message to His people. Taking each of these three steps will lead you to a statement of the heart of God's message.

Step One

The first step is to establish a truth sheet that answers the six basic questions, *who, what, where, when, why,* and *how.* You arrive at these answers going through the process of exegesis we have already noted. These statements of fact then lead to determining the principles in the text Each question seeks to bring out a particular kind of fact. As House and Garland say,

> "Answering the question, *who?* provides the *identification of persons.* Answering the question, *what?* discovers the *transaction* of any *performance.* "When" describes the *duration* of the *period* of time involved in the passage. By asking *where?* the *location* becomes the focus. The *causation of production* is discovered in answer to the question, *why?* Finally, answering the question, *how?* divulges the *function* of any *procedure* that may be described in the text." (Author's italics)[33]

Based on your study of the text, write answers to these questions.

Step Two

From the answers on the truth sheet write, a set of truths that combine the answers into truth statements that the passage teaches. There may be many of these. Not all of them are germane to the text being preached but are more general or accepted truths. After writing out as many as possible eliminate those not pertinent to the truth of the passage. This should result in two to six principles of truth that the author was teaching. "Principles should be stated as positive certainties of universal truth."[34]

A few cautions are in order. First, remember that these principles are "outstanding and abiding truths that are not limited to a moment in time."[35] Two things make a principle outstanding: It is prominent in the text, and it is also tied directly to the argument or story of the text. To be abiding, the principle must relate to any human circumstance in history.

Second, the form of the principle statement should be consistent with its outstanding and abiding nature. Don't use proper nouns. Compose positive statements rather than negative restrictions because positive statements reveal God's directive will. Each one should be a separate simple sentence.

Step Three

Next write the theme of the passage. This is comparable to Haddon Robinson's "a biblical concept" or "big idea."[36] This is the central point drawn from the passage's principles and stated in about nine words. The completed theme statement distills the principles you have drawn down to one sentence of a subject and predicate. The statement should be in terms that will have the greatest impact on the contemporary audience.

An Example of the Whiting Method

The following figure is an example of the three steps in the Whiting method.

This example is drawn from the preparation for a message on 2 Corinthians 1:1 – 11.

WHO? Paul, as a sufferer on behalf of all suffering believers.

WHAT? God permits suffering for believers because they are believers but also administers commensurate comfort through Christ.

WHERE? These are places of persecution or opposition to the practices of discipleship or ministry.

WHEN? At times when persecution happens, then the redemptive quality of suffering is used as comfort.

WHY? Paul's philosophy of suffering has played out to the Corinthians resulting in Paul's suffering and their encouraged faith. This is connected to the suffering of Christ.

HOW? Suffering for Christ and the Church is parallel with the comfort. Hence, what Paul suffered in Asia is redemptive, renewing and comforting for the church at Corinth.

PRINCIPLE STATEMENTS

God gives **grace, peace, pity and comfort** to those who **suffer** in **discipleship or ministry.**

God's gifts from **suffering** (above) are **mediated through pastoral experience** and example.

We **benefit** personally and corporately from suffering.

In the Christian meta-narrative, **suffering is redemptive.** In this case the redemption is effective in the church.

Christian **suffering anticipates resurrection.**

To face suffering, focus on the comfort by moving your confidence to God.

THEME

The pastor mediates grace, peace, pity and comfort to suffering disciples.*

*Note how the highlighted portions of the principle statements become the theme of the passage.

Sermon Notes for Review

A man once came to me and suggested that we sing all the verses of each hymn in the service. We had been singing only the verses that contributed to our theme for worship. He tried to add to his appeal by telling me that I would not have to study so much to find so much material to fill the time for the sermon. I told him that finding material to preach was not the problem. My biggest problem was discerning what material, out of all that I had learned, was most urgent to preach that Sunday to the congregation. The Whiting Method provides a series of steps that break down the exegetical information into principles and a theme statement. This theme statement can be the basis of the sermon to be preached.

What steps refine the results of study for sermon preparation?

1. Make notes of your study
2. Ask questions: Who? What? Where? When? Why? How?
3. Determine principles: two to six outstanding, abiding truths
4. Write a theme: a simple sentence summary of the principles

SUMMARY

When you determine the meaning of the text, you have the basis for developing the sermon and the text will dominate rather than your assumptions. The audience will hear the message of God rather than your thoughts. The meaning of the text is the basis of exposition. When you develop the expository sermon as described, it will give you confidence and will reach the small-church audience. First, the small-church audience will respond because of the obvious impact the Bible has on you, the preacher, and not because of your scholarship. Second the small-church audience will respond because the authority is derived from the text and not from a superior person or position or authority. Everyone will relate to the text equally thus substantiating their relationship to God.

PART 3
Teaching in a Small Church

In an informal survey I found that most small-church pastors don't describe themselves as preachers. They are more likely to identify themselves as teachers. According to Lori Carrell's more formal survey, the majority of preachers identify themselves as teachers.[37] This is only natural for preachers of expository sermons. The greatest struggle of an expository preacher will be to grasp and accurately communicate the content of the Bible.[38] Those who preach expository sermons must first be teachers. If you are beginning a ministry in a small church, this part will highlight the importance of teaching and reveal the purpose of teaching. This part will give any small-church pastor a format for teaching which accords with small-church characteristics.

CHAPTER 5
ON TEACHING AND PREACHING

Although this is a book about preaching in the small church, we cannot separate preaching from teaching. They have much in common and the Bible makes this connection clear: "Preach the word; be ready in season and out of season; reprove, rebuke, exhort, with great patience and instruction." (2 Timothy 4:2)

Before he looks at the degeneration of the church in future days, Paul gives a charge to Timothy. This charge follows hard on the declaration of the inspiration of Scripture (2 Timothy 3:16). The charge relates to how Timothy and all subsequent pastors must use this inspired Word.

The first verse of chapter 4 defines the conditions of the charge. Paul says the charge is solemn and he invokes God's sacred presence to the charge. All pastors need to realize that if we accept the charge that Paul is about to make, then what we have in the teaching and preaching of the Scriptures is not a toy; neither is it a tool to accomplish our personal or organizational ends. Though God may use it as a tool in people's lives, and He certainly will, it is not our tool to use as we think appropriate and to lay aside for other tools when it seems expedient. The communication of the Scripture is a sacred commission. All preaching is done before Jesus, and as such, carries His name. Therefore, He is the judge. His verdict, and not our own or the judgment of some other human, establishes preaching and its value for the church. Glenn O'Neal once suggested that when we stand up to preach, we should imagine that Jesus just slipped into a seat near the back. Our preaching and teaching should always honor Him.

In 2 Timothy 4:1 Paul also reminds us that our preaching is not finished nor is the effect fully registered until Jesus appears to institute His kingdom in its fullest form. Preaching goes in and out of favor as a trend among people. In some decades it is valued and sought, while in others it is despised. As this book is being written, preaching seems to be falling into a time of disfavor after a couple of decades of high interest. One reason is the preference for divided worship. The experience of the congregation singing music or watching others perform it is considered to be worship while preaching is merely added on to honor tradition. Another reason is the loss of confidence in universal truth. Since, as is currently thought, each individual perceives truth according to his or her own point of view and background, no one person can have anything authoritative to say to a collection of diverse individuals. Another cause is the presumption that no one can effectively communicate systematic knowledge about spiritual matters. In 2 Timothy 4:2 Paul directly opposes the concept of popular trends or culture making any changes in preaching and teaching. The value of preaching and teaching depends on the commission of God and on the universal and final kingdom of our Lord Jesus Christ.

The directive in verse two is at the heart of Paul's charge to Timothy and any who are called to preach. The command, "preach" is unequivocal. In Greek the verb is a gnomic aorist imperative, which tells us that preaching is an act we must do without concerning ourselves with repetition or subsequent sequence. It is a standard for behavior. When we consider the subsequent command to be ready in and out of season, the force of the aorist seems clear: We are to practice preaching without exception and without subjection to any other larger consideration. The standard for preaching is specified: the Word. This carries the sense of an absolute authoritative word as described in the context of 2 Timothy 3:16. So the preaching of the Word of God is not optional. It is not determined by societal factors such as acceptable forms of media or attention spans or dramatic experience. Expository preaching best meets the scriptural directive because it includes teaching in the course of exposition.

The preaching commanded in 2 Timothy 4:2 aims for life-change. Three aorist active imperatives expand the primary charge and give preaching the unique purpose of life-change. The first imperative, *reprove*, commands that preaching point out the wrong that the hearers are doing. The goal is conviction. The second, *rebuke* directs preaching to expose shameful behavior and seek to turn the hearers from activity that dishonors God. The third, *exhort* requires the sermon to encourage new behaviors that honor God and His righteousness. The picture of life-change is conviction, repentance and right behavior. This parallels the functions of the Scripture itself as declared in 2 Timothy 3:16 – 17. Three good effects of the Word are teaching, reproof and correction (3:16) like reprove, rebuke, and exhort (4:2.) It follows then that the one called of God would be adequate for the day, equipped and doing good works (3:17.) The charge to preach parallels these descriptions. It also argues for exposition as the best fulfillment of the charge.

According to 1 Timothy 4:2 two qualities will make preaching as effective as Paul commissions it to be. The first is a preacher quality - patience. Preaching must continue, but the fix will not be a quick one. Preaching will not bring a "happily ever after" ending. The story of sinners in need of repentance, renewal and direction does not end with one sermon. When Jesus conducted a preaching tour of the cities and villages of Galilee, His charge to the disciples reveals that more than just one tour would be required to meet the needs of those who were like sheep without a shepherd (Matthew 9:35 – 38.) The result was that He commissioned the Twelve to follow Him in His ministry. If Jesus preached with patience yet looked for results, the preacher today must exercise as Paul says, "all patience." Patience is "long suffering" or enduring in your passion for the task. If you aim to preach, you must passionately pursue the preaching with which you have been charged. As Alex Montoya says, "If there is no passion, there is no preaching."[39]

The Small Church and II Timothy 4:2

Many temptations entice small-church pastors away from the patient passion of preaching. When the church does not grow or lives don't show significant change after the pastor has preached, the temptation is to assume that there is something wrong with the preacher and give up. Because the results are not dramatic, many falsely assume that they are not "gifted" to preach, and so they fail to persist. Patient pursuit of the passion of preaching and teaching is required. Another common failure when preaching and seeing little result is to assume, therefore, that the congregation is too hardened to be affected by the sermon. Too many preachers give up and move to other congregations where they might have a more immediate and visible effect. Be patient. Another trap is to assume that the reason for less-than-dramatic responses to a sermon lies with the age or culture of the hearers. Thinking that modern listeners must be inured to old-fashioned preaching, some try a more modern message and abandon the singular charge to preach the Word. Others look for trendier methods that abandon the divine relationship that God established with His people from the beginning: He speaks and we listen. Patience with the method, the study, the delivery, the Bible, and the people is what makes preaching successful.

Small churches require extra patience. Because the small church is a network of relationships, and the preacher is usually an outsider, it takes patience to break into the circle of relationships. Acceptance and credibility are hard won, but no sermon will have its effect without them. Every small-church community has a set of values that are not written down in the bylaws. Until you can reflect those values, articulate them and incorporate them for comparison with the Scriptures your sermons will be suspect. Be patient. Finally, because small churches are isolated communities, they have a vocabulary of their own not shared with the majority society. You must learn to speak their language before your message is accepted and effective. Be patient. Some have suggested that in the small church, there are significant anniversaries in gaining ground with the congregation - three years, five years, seven years and beyond. At three years you get acceptance, at five years you gain influence and at seven years you move to leadership. It will take "all patience." Preach with patience.

Small-Church Teaching

While patience is the first characteristic that especially affects the small church, the second characteristic, teaching, governs the content. At the heart of expository preaching is information about the Bible. This information must be taught. You need to make the content of the Bible clear and explain its literary structure and grammar. Explore the interconnected quality of the books and passages of the Bible. Bring the backgrounds in history, culture, archaeology, linguistics, etc. to an understanding of the Bible. You do all these by teaching. You must study about the Bible before you can preach to people. Study is the preparation to teach and preach. Teaching must be part of the regular program of the church so that its members can bring a broad understanding of the Bible to each sermon. Learning about the Bible's contents benefits listeners when they hear a sermon about the Bible's directives. Before you can reprove, rebuke, and exhort from the Bible's message, you must teach about the Bible and its message in the course of the church ministry as well as in the course of the sermon.

Relationship of Teaching to Exposition

The expository sermon must incorporate sound teaching. This is done in three important ways: the use of Bible backgrounds, your explanation during the course of the sermon, and your application of the content of the Bible's text.

Bible backgrounds form a critical part of any good teaching. You must bridge the gap between the writer and readers of the ancient texts and your contemporary hearers. To do this explain Bible backgrounds in history, archaeology, geography, etymology, cultural anthropology and other subjects that bring the current hearers into the original context. For instance in 2 Corinthians 1:3 the phrase "God of all comfort" becomes clear when the Corinthian religious scene is understood. The Corinthians sought comfort for every manner of human ill from multiple gods in multiple temples. Paul brought a radical gospel of a God who was the God of *all* comfort. Expository sermons rely heavily on thorough teaching of Bible background material. This background material gives small-church listeners a context other than their own communities so they can understand the truth of the Bible.

In the course of the sermon you must explain the text's syntax, word meanings, and literary connections that make the writer's thoughts understandable. The vivid picture of Timothy's heritage from his mother and grandmother (2 Timothy 1:5) will help your audience understand the word *sincere* as relates to faith and would be a good text in a Mother's Day message. When listeners gain a biblical point of view on life in the course of an expository message, it opens them for life-change.

Accurate teaching, however, is more than simply giving information. You need to apply the biblical information to the listener's understanding concerning God, man, sin, the atonement, and all other categories of theology. Each passage contains insights into the biblical theology that the writer is communicating to his readers. When you apply information about the biblical text to these categories, the audience grows by understanding, at the point of exposition the concepts of theology as described in the Bible.

Richard Mayhue says, "Applying this idea to preaching requires that an expositor be one who explains Scripture by laying open the text to public view in order to set forth its meaning, explain what is difficult to understand, and make appropriate application."[40] Teaching comes before and is an integral part of preaching. When you study the text you gain understanding about the Bible so you can communicate it to the audience. Teaching is part of preaching because it is necessary to give the audience information about the Bible. Most small-church members are pleased to tell others that their pastor preaches from the Bible. Teaching that is integral to preaching affirms this value and wins the small-church audience. But preachers fail their commission when they seek merely to inform the frontal lobe.[41] The critical task of teaching lays groundwork for exposition.

Sermon Notes for Review

Country sages have long posed the question, "Which comes first, the chicken or the egg?" According to 2 Timothy 4:2 the priority for communication in the church is clear: good exposition builds on solid teaching. Teaching is the egg, and preaching is the chicken. The goal of teaching differs from that of preaching. The goal of preaching is life-change. The goal of teaching is gaining insights about the Bible by learning information about the Bible. Teaching must hold a place of authority in the small-church culture.

What is required for biblical communication at the small church?

1. Patience
2. Teaching

CHAPTER 6
ON TEACHING

Edna Sayer was a great evangelist. No, you will not see her name placarded with Billy Graham or D. L. Moody. Still, God gave her great fruitfulness as she led many boys and girls to Christ in the children's ministries of one small rural church. She, like many others of her type, taught Bible stories as the basis for her evangelism. Teaching the Bible is the basis of evangelism, discipleship and preaching.

Teaching in the Ministry of Jesus

When you look at Jesus' ministry, you see the primacy of teaching. Sixty-seven times Jesus is said to "teach", be "teaching" or have "taught." Everywhere He went, whether in the far reaches of Decapolis or near Galilee or in the temple at Jerusalem, teaching was His primary form of communication. Whether country folk or highly educated urbanites, they all received teaching from Jesus. When Jesus was on trial, He was tried for His teaching (John 18:19.) and defended His teaching (John 18:20). His teaching was so important to His ministry that when Luke summarizes Jesus' ministry at the beginning of Acts he says, "...all that Jesus began to do and to teach." (Acts 1:1) All observers agree, and Jesus Himself states it clearly: teaching has primacy.

However, Matthew notes that Jesus did more than teach. Teaching was the practice of the scribes and Pharisees and it was the chief activity in synagogue meetings. Describing Jesus' Galilean ministry, Matthew twice points to a special order in Jesus' approach. He says, "Jesus was ... teaching in their synagogues, and proclaiming the gospel of the kingdom, and healing every kind of disease..." (Matthew 4:23; 9:35) Teaching took priority in Jesus' approach. He taught as expected in a synagogue. But He went further. He also proclaimed the kingdom. Based on the teaching, He made an announcement of the Kingdom of God. The order of the three participles shows that Jesus based his proclamation and healing on teaching. He went further than the Rabbis. He not only gave explanation, but He also gave an announcement of the good news. His preaching was based on His teaching. In awe, His listeners recognized that what they received was something more than teaching (Mark 1:22).

Nowhere is this more apparent than in the brief excerpt that Luke gives us of Jesus teaching in the synagogue at Capernaum (Luke 4:16ff). Jesus read the scripture and then began the sermon in verse 21, "And He began to say to them, 'Today this Scripture has been fulfilled in your hearing.'" Initially the audience responded well to a teaching that they were to be the recipients of good news and liberation. Luke tells us, "all were speaking well of Him." However, when he began to reprove them by comparing them to Israel under God's judgment in the reign of wicked King Ahab, they became angry. So teaching about what Isaiah says was fine. This teaching was the basis of Jesus' sermon. However, when teaching turned to preaching, the crowd was offended. Jesus used teaching as the basis of His proclamation.

Teaching Among the Apostles

In practice the disciples followed Jesus' example of distinguishing teaching from a proclamation of the good news.

In Acts 2:42 the early church set a pattern of teaching as the primary activity when coming together. Preaching was built on solid teaching. In Acts 4:2 the soldiers of the Sanhedrin noted the distinction when observing the Apostles "teaching" and "proclaiming" among the people. As with Jesus, teaching came first; then a distinctive Christian announcement or proclamation followed. However, in Acts teaching remains the most common type of communication. The disciples were always telling the truths about Jesus for, initially, it was news to their hearers. This news was followed with a call to life-change in a sermon.

In the small church today the temptation is to move away from teaching as the basis of the preaching ministry of the church. Since the small church is characterized by personal relationships, it seems logical to abandon teaching for something more personal and less objective. Willimon and Wilson put it this way, "Preachers are misled into thinking that congregations want a personal testimony from them, rather than a witness to the testimony of the church, its scripture, and its tradition."[42] Teaching as the foundation of preaching moves the church from becoming a clique or a clan. Jesus' pattern, and that of the early church, should remain the pattern for the small church.

In the gospels the word used for teaching is *didasko* (A. T. Robertson's transliterations). The verb is used ninety-five times in the New Testament. At its heart the word means the transfer of knowledge from the teacher to the student by insight. In John 14:26, Jesus promises teaching by the Holy Spirit. However, the test of the Spirit's teaching is recall. So knowledge learned forms the main goal of teaching. Being able to recall that knowledge is the result of successful teaching.

The rabbis of Jesus day taught the Law in the synagogue so people would learn what they needed to reconcile with God and their neighbors. Teaching is communicating a body of knowledge to the student with the goal that the student will remember that data.

The apostle Paul taught often. Teaching was standard in his letters. He taught objective information about Christ and Christian belief that could be recalled. Eight times he called his readers to use the standard of his teaching to measure the truth of any other teaching. For example, in 2 Thessalonians 2:15 he exhorts the readers, "So, then brethren, stand firm and hold to the traditions which you were taught, whether by word of mouth or by letter from us." Clearly then, as Paul understood it, teaching communicated knowledge that could be used for comparison, evaluation, and decision. This is the work of biblical teaching. Biblical teaching communicates information about the Bible, Bible history, Bible characters, and Bible doctrine.

When Hebrews 5:12 says, "For though by this time you ought to be teachers, you have need again for someone to teach you the elementary principles..." the writer agrees with Paul's use of teaching - communicating objective information about the Bible. Such information is necessary. It is both foundational and forms a standard for evaluating all other communication. However it is different from preaching.

Teaching in the small church is no less essential than in larger churches. Teaching is foundational to preaching. What is needed in the small church is a means to teach that does not compromise the authority of the Scripture but adapts to the small-church congregation and its style. Teaching in the small church needs to conform to the biblical model. The teacher acquires knowledge about the Bible and then passes it on to the student through insight for the purpose of recall.

Sermon Notes for Review

Sitting in the small-church adult Sunday school class brings a very personal and familiar feel. As the class begins certain rituals must be performed. First there is a general round of greeting. This is followed by prayer. Then is the usual but grand entrance of the one member who is always late. A survey of the chairs is done. Then the inquiries about who is missing from the empty chairs must be done. Once the explanations of illness or travel, etc. have been recited, the class commences. As the class proceeds, regardless of the text or the questions being asked, there will be predictable responses from certain members of the class. You might assume that the ritual is vain. But teaching, even in the small church, is essential. The pattern of the Lord and the early church disciples cannot be given up. Preaching is based on good teaching. At the core of a sermon is information about the content of the Bible. This is biblical teaching that communicates information about the Bible.

When is teaching important?

1. When data about the Bible is needed.
2. When the authority of the Bible must be deferred to.
3. When the expository sermon is the goal.

CHAPTER 7
ON TEACHING IN THE SMALL CHURCH

When I graduated from seminary, my mind was filled with visions of delivering thrilling lectures to eager students. I had experienced that first hand. I had heard great men of the Word hold forth with sage understanding. They imparted gems of knowledge to me, and I resonated with their voices as I headed for my first church. I wanted nothing more than to have my congregation thrill to receive the sterling knowledge that I had stored so faithfully in those class notebooks now on my office shelves. I was shocked when they were not as thrilled as I had been - though admittedly there were a few gaps in the notes where I had apparently dozed off myself. I soon learned that the small church is not a lecture hall.

Teaching the Small Church

The intense, face-to-face relationships that characterize the small church mean that the academic distance created by a lecture approach will not work. It may even be offensive. Because the small church is a participatory democracy, you must allow for participation when you teach. However, the dynamic of the group cannot drive the teaching of the Bible. Teaching is communicating information about the Bible. Too much participation from your students can turn a teaching lesson into a study about the group and the member's favorite subjects.

My cousin had adult Sunday school classes with over 200 in attendance. The lecture format such as he was trained in at Dallas Theological Seminary obviously worked just fine. However, that size class is bigger than the largest church I ever served with Village Missions. A form of teaching that has worked well for me in these small places balances group involvement with input from the text. Keep in mind that most people learn best when they articulate the material they are learning. This is true for both children and adults. As people mature they usually move from manual to verbal articulation as the primary means of learning. So the small church is a very good setting, as are most small groups, for high quality learning. Since participation is important in a small church the best lesson structure allows you to teach authoritative biblical information and allows the students to participate as they understand and apply that information. Invite the group to study by involving the group members. You can clearly state the study's focus and read the relevant passages. Share information about the passage, including background information. Involve the group in an analysis of the text. Finally, draw a personal application. These then are the five parts of the lesson: approach, focus, information, analysis, and personal application. We begin with the focus to build the lesson plan.

The Focus of the Lesson

After you do the exegesis of the passage by your most reliable system or the one described in chapter two, make the passage's central point the focus of the lesson. This focus is the theme you will teach in the course of the lesson. All the material that you develop for the lesson plan should in some way serve this theme.

State the focus of the lesson in a single, simple sentence. If the sentence has the word *and* or *but* in the middle, it becomes a compound sentence. Simplify that focus to a single, simple sentence. If it seems necessary to teach both parts of a compound sentence from one passage then make two lessons for the passage, each with its own simple-single-sentence focus. A sentence with too many relative clauses is too complex for the focus of the class. "Since the fall, when Eve took the forbidden fruit and Adam failed to intervene, man has had to both contend with what modern science calls the Second Law of Thermodynamics in the deterioration of the earth's resources and create a livelihood out of an unhealthy environment." This focus statement is too complex to give the core of a lesson on Genesis 3:17 - 21. It would be better to say, "The fall affects our work today" or "The fall creates man's work environment." Either of these focus statements allows you to develop the lesson's supporting material from the text while avoiding extraneous material that will divert the audience. Alternatively, if the lesson describes a truth in the Bible you may state the focus as a heading rather than a complete sentence, "The effects of the fall."

The following are some examples of texts and the focus statements for those texts

- Acts 9:36 – 40   Prayer and resurrection power
- Ezra 3:1 – 6   A cry to God is framed in obedience
- Luke 5:16   Jesus is a model of prayer
- I Thessalonians   Support the ministry of your Village
  5:12 – 13   Missionary
- I Corinthians   Encourage church leadership to work
  10:32 – 33   together
- Psalm 78   Fathers fail or fulfill their roles

The Approach to Draw the Audience into the Lesson

Once, when teaching a group of new missionaries in a training course, I brought a lesson that seemed to draw high interest from the students. Later I taught the same lesson to an adult Sunday school class. The interest reached such a peak as to provoke a yawn. I forgot to measure the potential audience interest. The first class of new missionaries had to learn this material, and it made sense in the larger course it was part of. The subsequent adult Sunday school class had no inkling of why I taught the lesson or how it related to them. I failed to develop a good approach. The approach to the lesson creates this sense of connection and gives it vitality for the student.

It is best to form an approach after you write the focus of the lesson. Then you know what the student is being drawn to. Sometimes it is better to write the approach after you complete the whole lesson. Then you can craft the approach with precision to lead to the study and personal applications. In any case the approach must give sense to the lesson, create relevance for the study and give credence to the focus statement.

In the course of teaching any small group, there will be routines that may form part of the approach to the lesson. These could include personal sharing, news of events, prayer, or singing. Each of these can form part of the lesson's approach. Some groups naturally include singing of Christian songs as their opening. These songs can be selected to relate to the focus of the lesson. You can use the lyrics of one or two songs to introduce the focus. Informal prayer may suggest a need that the lesson will address. You can ask someone to share a particular need or answer to prayer that connects to the lesson. General questions can provoke personal sharing. You can ask, "Have you ever had the experience of...?" or "When you encounter ... what is your reaction?" This works especially well in a small church where people share the same experiences. They will share readily, and that will encourage their participation throughout the lesson. The thoughts or reactions they relate may vary, but the direction of the Scripture in the lesson will speak to those thoughts. Drawing the group in to compare their story with the counsel of Scripture will make a good approach.

For a number of years I had the responsibility of presenting the morning devotion to a summer conference staff. This small group of program leaders was responsible for making everything come together each day of conference. All the staff members had experience as small-church pastors. The conference was for small-church pastors. To highlight the need to love and engender love during the conference, the approach I used to a lesson on 1 Corinthians 13:13 was to ask them to recall what people remembered about former pastors. After they shared I noted that the love and care they received topped the list. In a lesson series, "Prayer in the life of Christ" I used prayer as an approach to a lesson for Matthew 8:1 – 4. I asked each person to pray for another in the group. Then I asked them to tell about someone they regularly pray for. The focus for that lesson was "Prayer that is direct is heeded." The approach should lead to the focus. Establish the focus of the lesson first so that your approach may lead to the focus in a relevant way. When you write the lesson to guide the class, the approach comes first, followed by the focus.

Information

The next section of the lesson plan gives the backgrounds and important information about the passage. This is your sole responsibility as teacher. Base the information section on the exegesis of the passage that you do in the course of your study.

The information section should outline the backgrounds of the text. This should include the information about the book, the author, and the readers. Help your students locate the book in the Bible and explain the contribution that it makes to biblical theology. Information on history, culture, archaeology and geography is part of the information section. The author's biography is very important for students to grasp. It would be difficult to understand the urgency of Second Timothy without knowing the Apostle Paul's end-of-life scenario. As a teacher you will provide linguistic and literary considerations that form part of the background information. For example, the nature of Hebrew poetry and Isaiah's high literary style help the student to grasp his message. It is important to communicate book structure to the students. The chiastic structure of much of the Old Testament applies differently to the various books of the Old Testament. The spiraling logic of First John is important to understand and apply in the lesson from any given text in First John.

However, you won't share all of this information in each lesson. For a series of lessons on the same book of the Bible, the amount and specifics of the information section of the lesson will change. In the initial lessons you will share more information, such as a greater amount of the broad background of the book. This would include such things as geography and author biography or the readers' faith history and culture. In subsequent lessons you will review pertinent information. When teaching from First John review the book's spiraling logic with each lesson to understand how the current text repeats and expands on the author's basic themes. When teaching on Jeremiah, for each lesson you'll need to update the changing historical scene out of which the prophet writes. You will add more detail to the initial information on the book at each lesson including particular linguistic or literary considerations for the specific text under study.

You, the teacher, have this information and must inform the students. This is a one-way communication: teacher to student. In a small-church context this may seem counterproductive because small churches are by nature participatory. One-way communication that limits participation can offend small-church students. However, this is necessary for the spiritual health of any church. God has spoken to people in every context of the human condition, not just to the members of the small church and their society. The information section of a lesson calls the students to bow before the authority of Scripture. It is important for the teacher in the small church not to lord it over the students but to use inclusive language saying that we all need to know this information to understand God's message to us. Small churches are usually democracies. Again the information section of a lesson may prove offensive to this democratic ethic. However, small-church classes need to be reminded that the authority of the Bible holds us accountable to God and not the reverse. You can add a sense of participation and democracy by asking students to read the text, read cross references, or review previous lessons. You can also ask the student specific and leading questions that bring out background information. The information section of the lesson is important for you to develop fully and give to the students.

Analysis

While student participation in the information section of the lesson is minimal, the analysis section of the lesson invites participation. In analysis, everyone hears the student's thoughts and conclusions. However, the class remains teacher guided. The analysis section of the lesson is not about the student nor about the teacher but is a means to ascertain God's message to us in the Bible.

To lead the analysis section of the lesson prepare an outline of the text based on a breakdown of the thought units. So the outline should flow from the text and parallel the development of the logic of the text. The purpose of the outline is to bring the students into contact with the author's thought and intents. In the course of the lesson analysis you will read or have someone read the portion of the text according to the outline. You may give some summary comments about how the text, which has been read, connects with the context and development of thought. Then you invite the students to comment on the text.

Student participation should develop the text in two ways.

The students should articulate God's message as presented by the author. Then they attach meaning or implication to the text. In their own words the students need to say what the author is saying. By doing this the students are bringing the text out of the ancient world and into the current context. This practice opens the door for relevancy to the students' lives. You may elicit this relevancy in a variety of ways. You could simply ask, "How would you say this in your own words?" Or you could ask the person on the student's right to whisper the Bible's message in the text to the student on his or her right. By the time all the whisperings are repeated around the circle, it will be a complete paraphrase of the text. Establishing a paraphrase is the objective.

The second objective is to establish a meaning for the text. You direct the students to extract from the text and the paraphrase what the meaning is for us in our context. You want to draw out the implications for faith and conduct in the lives of the class members today. You may simply ask, "What does this mean for us?" Or, "To whom would you apply this text today and how would you apply it?" Use open ended questions such as *Why? How?* or *What?* Whatever the answers may be, you reinforce the meanings that are consistent with the thought unit of the text and its context. You may do this by simply summarizing the best elements of several meaning-statements made by students. You may also say, "The text says, '.....' but you put it differently. Why?" Then follow that student's reasoning by asking the other students what they think. Then again you summarize the comments closest to the text's meaning. Note that this process keeps the comments tied to the text. Do this for each unit of thought in the analytical outline of the text. A worksheet may be helpful. Worksheets ask students to note their thoughts in advance of the discussion. This can save time. You can encourage the more reticent students to participate by sharing what they have written on their worksheets.

In a small church, participation is encouraged and everybody's contribution is valued. This leads to awkward moments for the teacher. When a student's paraphrase of the text or the meaning drawn from it is far from the message of the text, you cannot say, "Wow! That's stupid." But there are other ways to turn the discussion. In using any means to turn the conversation, remember that it is always your goal to turn the conversation back to the text. When an "off the wall" comment comes up, say something such as, "Hmmm, I wouldn't have thought of it that way but the text says, '...' What do some of the rest of you say?" In any case you should use as much restatement, reinforcement, and approval as possible. In restatement you should try to highlight the aspects of the comment that contribute to the correct direction of the discussion when you restate the comment. When reinforcing a good contribution, note the best of that contribution. You might say, "I like that thought. Does anyone have anything to add?" Approval is much stronger. Approval confirms that the comment is accurate, "That is a good point and exactly parallels the text in this way." To avoid trouble, establish the discussion as participatory and the rule that all contributions will be accepted. But use positive direction also to establish that the text rules over the comments of both teacher and student alike.

Personal Application

As you develop the lesson, each previous section leads to the next section. Personal application is the logical end of this process. In personal application you ask the students to conclude how they can put this text into action in their daily circumstances. The lesson's personal application section continues the class's high level of democratic participation that agrees with the ethic of the small church. Encourage verbal participation and welcome all such contributions.

While you ask the students how they would apply the passage, you still have a directive role in their comments. First, you summarize the analysis for the entire discussion. In some class settings you can facilitate that by using a chalkboard, white board or other medium. The larger class size, the longer the class time or the more lengthy passages of Scripture being discussed will require you to keep some record of the discussion so you can summarize it in preparation for the personal application. In the summary, you take the thought-units of the text and briefly state a condensation of the meanings for those sections.

After you summarize, ask the students to state the ways they could foresee putting this into action. The average student has a hard time envisioning these actions. Most are used to the application of the usual disciplines of Bible reading and prayer. You should be prepared to direct students to consider other possibilities. In addition to the above prayer and Bible reading the students could apply the text to faith. You could ask, "How must I change my beliefs?" and encourage the students to think differently because of God's message. You can encourage them to apply the text more specifically to finances, relationships, work ethic, communication, goal setting, etc. In a less directive approach you will simply ask for suggestions for applying the text to relationships or other areas. In a more directive approach you will give an assignment to carry out the application in the context of some daily activity and report back the following week.

Formatting the Lesson

Build the lesson format as suggested above. Complete the exegesis of the passage. Then develop the passage's central point or theme on the basis of your study. Convert that central point to the focus of the lesson. The central point of the passage is usually stated in biblical or theological terms. State the focus in terms of the lives of the students. This single, simple sentence should be the basis for what you develop in the remainder of the passage. This sentence states the core of the study concerning what the biblical text says about a subject. For this reason the *focus* comes first in the lesson development. However, in the format for presentation the *focus* is the second item.

The *approach* to the lesson is the first item in the order of the lesson format, while it is second in lesson development. The approach should prepare the students for the lesson's focus. Therefore, plan the approach so it will interest them in the lesson's topic. This can be a story, an exercise, or a question for discussion. In the small church the more participation you bring out in the approach the better the lesson will be received by the class members. The questions which invite sharing in the approach will set the tone for the rest of the lesson.

The *focus* is the second part of the lesson plan. Though you develop it from the theme of the Scripture and it governs the entire lesson plan, stating the focus when you present the lesson has the best effect when you lead up to it by the approach to the lesson.

Information is the third item in the lesson format. It explains what the student must understand before they can grasp the meaning in the text as it relates to the subject in the *focus* statement. The *information* section covers significant background and other explanatory material that you produce. You will lecture, however briefly, on data the students need to know so they can prepare to participate in the discussion. The lesson plan's *information* section helps control the discussion because it excludes extraneous opinions by limiting the discussion to a literal understanding of the text.

The *analysis* section of the lesson plan begins when you invite students to explore and discuss the flow of thought in the biblical text as you have outlined it. Through various means help the class members bring out a re-statement of the text. Also ask for the student's conclusions about the text's meaning and implications for people today. Encourage everyone to participate and allow all comments. However, you will use positive restatements, reinforcements, and approval to direct the comments to agree with the text. This is a discussion section in the lesson plan. It is a good place for students to complete worksheets that help them ask questions about the meaning of the text and that give them thought-out insights to share with the class.

Finally the lesson concludes with *personal application* - an action plan. During discussion, class members come up with the plan to give them direction so they can act out the text in the course of daily life.

The lesson plan format is as follows:

» Approach
» Focus
» Information
» Analysis
» Personal application.

Time is a key factor in the lesson plan's development. A two-hour Bible study allows for much discussion and varying formats to encourage participation. For example, a two hour Bible study allows time to let the class share personal stories or observations in the approach. A longer text and the reading of a longer context are good to begin the long study. You can be more detailed in the information section of the lesson plan for a lengthy study. You can look up many cross references with the class and linger over the analysis section. You can encourage the class to do different exercises to encounter the text and discern the meaning. You can give more time to comments by all class members. In the personal application part of the lesson you can allow students to discuss action plans that may be quite complicated or involve a large scope of activity.

However, in a ten minute devotional the same format will work. But some things will have to be shortened greatly. The approach you offer will be from experiences or observations common to the class. You'll have to limit the information section to just the information that is salient to the text under consideration. For example, to grasp the urgency of Peter's reminders in 2 Peter 1:12 and following, it would be essential to point out Peter's imminent death at the hands of Nero and his experience on the Mount of Transfiguration. The analysis should not allow for free-ranging discussion and you should limit open-ended questions. Any questions you ask may have to be rhetorical only. The action plan you offer in the personal application will have to be specific and allow no discussion in order to complete a lesson plan in ten minutes.

Sermon Notes for Review

You can blend authoritative teaching of information about the Bible with the participatory discussion favored by small churches. You can teach small-church Bible studies using the format described above: approach, focus, information, analysis, personal application. In one church I pastored, each weekly prayer meeting began with a Bible study in Ezra. We looked at Ezra's difficult times and circumstances. We discussed what that meant for us. Then we prayed for one another, for the church, and for our missionaries. You can match the need for relationship and participation in the small church with the teaching of the scriptures using the format above.

What lesson format allows for biblical teaching and group participation?

1. Approach.
2. Focus.
3. Information.
4. Analytical.
5. Personal application.

SUMMARY

Teaching...
- ... is essential to the ministry of the small church.
- ... communicates objective information about the Bible.
- ... is a biblical example
- ... is a mandate for all churches including the small church, and
- ...undergirds expository preaching.

People need to know information about the Bible before they can grasp its message. They get this through effective teaching. Expository preaching must include teaching about the Bible in the course of the sermon to make the message of the text understandable and effective for life-change. This is why Paul admonishes Timothy to preach with teaching (2 Timothy 4:2.) Yet teaching that is done as an authoritative act by the knowledgeable and superior to the ignorant and inferior does not match small-church characteristics. The right lesson plan will structure the lesson to draw its source of information from the Bible and let the message of the Bible govern the participation in discussion.

PART 4
Outlining the Sermon

"What did you preach on last Sunday?" asks a fellow pastor at the weekly prayer breakfast. While you can recall the passage, the outline is illusive. When you're not able to remember the outline you feel a sense of pity for your congregation and you wonder how they would do if asked the same question. Of course the goal of teaching is recall, but the goal of preaching is life-change. Whether your audience remembers the main points of your message, let alone the sub-points, is not the goal. The way to effect life-change in the small church is to use a sermon structure that capitalizes on the characteristics of the small church. The *problem-question* format in sermon structure allows the expository message to best meet the characteristics of small-church dynamics. If you are preaching in a small church, whether you have preached for years or are just now entering the pulpit, this section provides a means to expound the Scriptures in the small-church context. It explains the value of the problem-question format, it explains the how to structure this type of sermon, and it gives types and examples of problem-question sermons.

CHAPTER 8
PROBLEM QUESTION

Problem-Question as a format for homiletic structure was taught for years by Alva J. McClain at Grace Theological Seminary.[43] Later Glenn O'Neal, one of McClain's students taught the problem-question or problem-solution format at Talbot Theological Seminary. In his textbook, *Make the Bible Live* O'Neal describes the process of preparing the outline. He recommends that after determining the meaning of the passage, you state a unifying thrust for the message based on that meaning. To do this, ask yourself, "What purpose can be accomplished in the lives of the people which are in harmony with the intent of the selected portion of Scripture?"[44] The intent of the passage – the sermon's unifying thrust - should be stated as a question. O'Neal continues, "The next step is to state the problem carefully, making sure that each word is the most meaningful, and that the idea is presented in a concise manner. It is best to state the problem in the form of a question or an incomplete sentence."[45]

The problem-question format does not compromise the place of preaching. The Bible is clear; preaching is a sacred task that the church must promote and uphold until the Lord returns. The temptation of the day is to replace preaching with other means to inspire and direct the church. An infatuation with technology, a loss of confidence in truth, and a focus on the felt needs of people has led to preaching in the church being displaced by other media and messages.[46] For small churches some recommend dialogue-based or congregation-based approaches to sermon structure that would abandon historic preaching and set aside the authority of the Scriptures. The problem-question format maintains the authority of the Bible through preaching. Because the question is at the heart of this structure, the Bible rises in authority as the only answer and the Word of God and His message to His people are heard clearly. A problem-question sermon sounds like a traditional sermon. It validates the tradition of preaching that the church has cherished.

The problem-question format is expositional in nature because the preacher answers the question from the Bible text. The points of the text form parts of the answer to the problem-question. At the end of the sermon, the central point of the text becomes a call to life-change. O'Neal goes on, "This forces you to unify the main points of the sermon by having each point either answer the question or complete the sentence. It is impossible to separate the task of stating the problem from that of determining the points of the outline. The thoughts taken from the passage which become the main points of the outline must answer the question asked in the problem."[47]

The Value of a Problem-Question Sermon

A few of the many books on preaching even mention the problem-question format. If they do, they often dismiss it as redundant and juvenile. However, a closer consideration will give a broader picture of the usefulness of the problem-question format particularly in the small church.

First, the text dictates the content of the problem-question message. Paul said to preach the Word. Nothing else can be as powerful and authoritative as preaching to God's people the message of God as found in the Bible. It is so easy to get an idea from the Bible but have your own thoughts, the world's wisdom, or the audience's needs become the source of the preaching. The problem-question ultimately asks a question of the text and only the text may answer it. This is the heart of evangelical, reformation preaching. Martin Luther called for the Scriptures alone to stand in authority over God's people. Using a problem-question format holds the preacher to that tradition. If you begin to insert your own thoughts, if you hold up the world's wisdom as authoritative it is obvious to all. The Bible is the unifying point of identity between you and the congregation. This is especially true in small churches where the preacher is an interloper in the small-church web of relationships. The problem-question format gives common ground to you and the congregation as mutual questioners of the text. The exposition of the text answers the question.

Second, questions are the basic means of study. When you spend hours in study, you are asking questions of the text. You may ask, "Where does this thought come from?" or "What does this word mean here?" or "How do these ideas fit together?" These, along with many other questions, are the basis of study. Study is inquiry. This is as it should be. Nearly every book on preaching that includes directions on study, including this one, directs the preacher to question the text. The problem-question format lets the congregation in on this study process. They are asked to join you in discovery of the Bible's answers rather than revere you as the Bible-answer person. This is consistent with the democratic nature of relationships in the small church. Furthermore, this format reinforces what pastors constantly direct their people to do - ask their questions of the Bible.

Third, the problem-question format levels the relationship between you and the audience. The small church has little value for relationships based upon position but a great value for relationships based on common experience. The use of the problem-question format opens the door for growing shared experience as both you and the audience answer the question together. Certainly the pastor has greater skill in studying the Bible and presenting the message, but greater skill and superior position are different. The audience will benefit from your greater skill as they follow you in the unfolding of the Bible's answer to the question. Consistent use of this format builds recognition of your skill. Over time the congregation grants authority to one who has demonstrated skilled faithfulness to the Word of God. During announcements at one small church I pastored, a faithful board member stood and exhorted people to attend Sunday evening saying, "We're just a model T church with a Cadillac pastor who teaches the Bible with power on Sunday nights." I was flattered to think that I had gained that kind of credibility using this method. While an intern was making a point during his sermon one Sunday he closed his fist and jabbed his index finger at the congregation. He paused, "I may have one finger pointing at you but I've got three pointing at me."

Fourth, the problem-question format upholds the authority of Scripture for preacher and parishioner alike. The question is asked by all who take God's Word seriously. The conviction of the Holy Spirit falls evenly on all who take the question seriously - which was the intern's point. The practice of using the problem-question format leaves the door open for scriptural pastoral care. When providing comfort or guidance to someone in crisis or pain, the same mutual submission to the authority of Scripture unites the shepherd and the sheep as they approach the Bible seeking God's counsel and mercy.

Fifth, the problem-question sermon structure invites the congregation members to join you in finding the answer to the question. This heightens the sense of relationship between members of the audience themselves as well as between you and the audience. Furthermore, this sermon structure is participatory by design. In other forms of sermon development the audience can see the logic and relevance of your insights. In the problem-question format the answer develops through the points of the sermon that the text supplies. The audience members take these points as their answer, saying such things, silently or aloud as, "Aha! Yes! I agree." They participate in the uncovering of God's answer for themselves. In so doing they have a heightened sense of anticipation. Good listeners try to anticipate the preacher's next thought but the problem-question format forces this practice of good listening by not giving a conclusion about the Bible message as the main point or big idea of the sermon. Instead it presents a question to be answered.

Sixth, the problem-question format initiates a conversation about the answers in the Scripture. In the course of answering the question, the audience is agreeing, disagreeing, confirming, denying, affirming and applying the answers with the pastor – at least mentally. This natural dialogue between the preacher and the audience doesn't have to be forced by some sermon format that ignores the authority of Scripture. Instead, the problem-question format invites this dialogue. Responses can be verbal. Traditionally congregation members have said, "Amen!" from time to time as part of this dialogue. But the dialogue carries on mentally and sometimes verbally throughout the message.

The seventh virtue of the problem-question format is that it models the best form of Bible study, inductive Bible study. While pastors routinely teach their congregations to study the Bible inductively, the sermon is usually deductive. In most sermons the pastor states the thesis and then lays out the substantiation of the thesis as the points of the sermon. This sets the pastor apart as the expert and suggests that the pastor's reasoning is superior. It seems to say to church members that they must study inductively but pastors can study deductively. The problem-question lets the Bible speak. The thesis of the text is summed up as the answer to the question and a call for action. This encourages each of the members of the congregation to study the Bible inductively.

Eighth, the problem-question format leads the congregation

to take ownership of the answer to the question. When you ask the problem-question, the sermon forms a contract with the audience to discover the answer. As the audience discovers the parts of the answer through the points of the message, they are inclined to take them as their own since they discovered them. In Matthew 13:44 Jesus illustrated the way that discovery leads to ownership. He says, "The kingdom of heaven is like a treasure hidden in the field, which a man found and hid; and from joy over it he goes and sells all that he has, and buys that field." Note that what is discovered has value to the discoverer. It causes him to rejoice and to bank the treasure away. Then he gives up every thing to gain the kingdom. This is the process the problem-question seeks to stimulate. The value of discovering of the answers to the question motivates us to take ownership in a way that can be realized only by giving up everything for the kingdom of God. The problem-question format appeals to the high sense of ownership in the small-church congregation.

As a ninth virtue, the problem-question is a natural setting for other forms of audience participation. The pastor of the church I currently attend expounds the Scripture deductively. In the course of the message he asks rhetorical questions. He is shocked when Kevin answers from the balcony. Actions during a sermon in the problem-question format, such as looking up a verse or nodding one's head or other actions, are perfectly natural and expected. Verbal responses are normal in this highly participatory kind of sermon format. Furthermore, responses that the preacher seeks in the conclusion of the sermon follow logically. Most pastors end a sermon with a summary of the main points they initially asserted and now have eruditely proven. They may follow with some suggestions of how the audience can implement the message, but more often, as I have noticed in my long experience of listening to sermons, they end with a prayer for God to "seal" it to our hearts. But with a problem-question format, once the question is discovered, then, like the man in Matthew 13:44, the listener is inclined to take direction from the preacher to put off some things or give them up and to take on others in their place.

Finally, your example as one who wrestles with the Word of God becomes more vivid and valued. The problem-question format will open the opportunity for you to share some of your personal doubts, questions and struggles to understand and apply the Word of God. Sometimes you will be able to express your enthusiasm over your own discoveries in the study and application of the Word. But you are just as likely to be transparent about your failures. This kind of honesty builds a relationship with the congregation. Your sermons explain your example in the way you live your life. In a small church, people not only know what you do, but they also know what you do well and not so well. The problem-question format allows for personal testimony of confirmation or conviction that unites your life and your preaching. Your *ethos* will be built. In a small church which values relationship more than image, this unifying process is powerful to drive the message home with the force of reality.

Problem-Question is Best for the Small-Church Context

Small churches provide a unique context for preaching. Most training on preaching assumes that the preacher, the audience, and the Bible are all fixed commodities. The Bible is given by inspiration from God and is not subject to our manipulation. It is fixed. The audience is not a malleable commodity. Since all audiences are human and sinners, they remain a fixed commodity of human nature. So the best point to effect any change in preaching is in the preacher. You are the only one who submits yourself to training. You are the only one who will perhaps buy this book. But these assumptions, including the last, are wrong. The congregation is not a fixed commodity in the business of preaching. Most books on preaching, including this one, urge the preacher to analyze the audience and then preach to that audience. This implies that there are characteristics that vary with varying audiences at varying times. Certainly the small church has characteristics that set it apart from the medium or large church. These are known characteristics. (See chapter one.) When you preach a sermon in a problem-question format it works effectively to move the small-church audience to life-change because you have declared God's message in the Bible. The problem-question format for a sermon is the format that matches best with the characteristics of the small church.

Small churches do not grant position apart from relationship. A position of authority or influence does not come with a letter of recommendation. It doesn't result from the endorsement of a pulpit committee or a congregation. These things matter and help in getting one started in a pulpit ministry but the small-church congregation's relationship with you as a minister of the gospel grows according to your ability to let the preaching become a standard for the church family's spiritual life.

This puts expertise on the second shelf below relationship. The small church will be flattered and even take pride at having attracted a pastor with acknowledged expertise in theology, biblical studies, or homiletics. Yet until that pastor is brought into the circle of the church family, the pastor's influence will be minimal. A way to view the small church is as a family with parental figures such as patriarch and matriarch.[48] One Episcopal study of churches of various sizes concluded that the family church of fifty members or fewer will have parental figures that sanction or adopt newcomers into the church. When the priest or deacon comes to the church, these same parental figures sanction the role of chaplain to the family for that pastor.[49] It is the relationship structure, not the position, that determines power, influence, and authority. A sermon structure such as the problem-question format works because it is permissive. The problem-question sermon seeks permission to influence these parental figures and the entire church family. This approach, while granting place and position to these parental figures, invites them to respond as fellow inquirers in the search for the answer to the problem-question.

Audience participation comes from a high sense of ownership. The buildings, grounds, and ministries of the small church are in most cases the fruit of the giving and labor of generations of the same families. This gives the present generation a sense of ownership. A sermon's problem-question format appeals to that sense of ownership. People respond by participating in the search for the answers, and they own the resulting answers. The problem-question format, more than any other type of format best builds the sense of ownership that is based on a small-church's ethic of participation.

Small churches are anti-authoritarian. While they often highly value good citizenship and support the government and the military, they do not submit easily to those who use authority. Members of the small church react to dictatorial or directive authority based upon position or expertise. These people are independent. In many instances they have resisted the trend to migrate with most Christians to a larger more programmatic church. Small church values of quality, face-to-face relationships have held these people in the small church. They naturally resist external authority. Because the problem-question sermon format draws authority from the Bible by virtue of the question, it diverts the small church's inherent resistance to human authority.

On an air flight I was seated next to a pilot who was returning home near Chicago after finishing his flight shift for the airline. He told me his story of growing up in a small church in a small town area outside Chicago. About the time he married, he began to attend Willow Creek Community Church with Pastor Bill Hybels. He attended there for several years and became acquainted with the church's staff and ministries by serving in several volunteer capacities. However, when his children were born, and began to grow, he and his wife elected to return to the small church in which he grew up. He said it was because he wanted his children to have the same face-to-face relationship with the pastor and other members of all generations that he had benefited from in his childhood. The problem-question sermon structure agrees with this kind of small church value.

For the small-church member authority is not based on knowledge. Certainly the staff at Willow Creek is knowledgeable and has many published works, but my airline acquaintance and his family did not submit their authority to knowledge. Credentials are not the basis for authority in the small church. Though the staff at Willow Creek has well-known and respected credentials, for my airline acquaintance that credentialing was outweighed by their relationship with the pastor. The same is true for chain-of-command and performance. Neither of these one dimensional relationships are the basis of authority in the small church. My airline acquaintance did not choose the small church and its pastor because they lacked these things but because the relationship was holistic, and multi-dimensional. He was willing to submit to authority that is known and by which he and his family could be known.

In summary the problem-question format for sermon structure builds its authority on relationship. This format preserves the authority of the Bible. It is clearly expositional in that it exposes God's message to His people. But the message's authority derives from the sermon's invitation implicit in the central problem-question for the pastor and congregation to relate together in searching for the answers in God's Word. In this search the pastor is known and the congregation participates. For this reason it is an outstanding format for the small-church context.

Sermon Notes for Review

After a year of expounding Hebrews, Lila shook my hand on the way out the door. She said, "When you first came and began preaching on Hebrews I didn't get it. But now I'm discovering more each Sunday." The problem-question turns the theme of the passage that you find through exegesis, into a question for your congregation to answer as you lead them in the sermon. This format best suits the characteristics of the small church while keeping the authority of the Bible foremost in preaching.

What are three advantages of the problem-question format for the small church?

1. It creates relationship with the congregation.
2. It invites ownership by the congregation.
3. It stimulates small-church participation by the congregation.

CHAPTER 9
FORMATING THE PROBLEM-QUESTION SERMON

The Ryrie Study Bible notes the central point for Isaiah 28:16.[50] Assuming that this point is the result of legitimate exegesis, the central point of the text could be stated, "The Messiah is Israel's Rock." The subsequent points of the text are, "A foundation stone in atonement," "A test stone in temptation," and "A costly cornerstone for His people." The central point of the text converts to the big idea for the sermon. Using a problem-question format you would restate the central point as a question.

Frame the Question

Framing the question for a problem-question sermon requires careful wording. You arrive at the best wording by stating and re-stating the question. Begin with the central point of the text that you derive from careful exegesis, and ask the question of the text For Isaiah 28:16, the question could be stated as a literary question, "In what ways does the promised Messiah fulfill the type of a rock to Israel?" This is an impersonal and purely academic question. The answer will not tell the listener anything about the Messiah or about the human condition. It would be better to restate the question, "How is the Messiah Israel's rock?" In the answer to this question, each type of stone in Isaiah 28:16 gives us a picture of the Messiah. The relevance to Israel is apparent. The Messiah will make Israel both strong and stable.

In the answers to the above question, each point comprises part of the answer. Each point from the text should give a picture of the Messiah and the relation to Israel. The first point, "He is a foundation stone in the atonement," points out that Israel's relation to God is stable through the atonement as a once-for-all act fulfilling the covenant with God. The second point, "He is a test stone in temptation," relates the Messiah as their strength when Israel is tempted. The third point, "He is a costly cornerstone," shows the measure of Christ's sacrifice as precious and of immense value for His people. Each point should be a piece of the answer. The whole should be summed up as an answer. "Israel can trust the Messiah because His atonement provides a stable relationship with God, a hope and bulwark against temptation, and great wealth of forgiveness and mercy paid for by His sacrifice." However, as this answer sums up the points it also makes obvious the lack of audience connection for most small churches. It would need to be revised for the small church congregation.

Frame the Question for the Audience

Once you have stated the biblical problem-question then you need to go back and restate this same question in audience terms. This step has a few qualifiers. One is your connection with the audience in terms of our fallen human nature. Another is generalizing the subject to one that the biblical audience and the contemporary audience would have in common.

Bryan Chappell has given expositors a redemptive connection between the text and the contemporary audience with the concept of the "Fallen Condition Focus."[51] He writes, "The Fallen Condition Focus (FCF) is the mutual condition that contemporary believers share with those to or about whom the text was written..." Before you can write the problem-question in audience terms you must determine the fallen condition of the biblical people that is common with your own audience. To establish this you must review what the text says, for that will establish specific conditions addressed. Then, in a more specific way you must determine the concerns the text has for change in its original audience. Now, as you prepare the problem-question, you list the ways the current audience is also subject to the concerns the text has for those to whom or about whom it was written. This establishes the negative condition from which the text challenges the audience to turn and make significant life-change. When you write a problem-question with this fallen-condition focus in mind, it leads the audience to answers in the text that challenge them to repentance and renewal.

Don Sunukjian addresses a second consideration in framing the problem-question. He has given expositors the ladder of abstraction.[52] The Bible is very particular about times, people, circumstances and events. All of these long-ago, far-away and very different circumstances seem to leave out the situation of the contemporary audience. But by climbing the ladder of abstraction to descriptions consistent with the text but sufficiently broad to describe things in this century, you can write the problem-question to challenge the contemporary audience.

Refer back to the Isaiah 28:16 passage and the outline already stated for a problem-question. The fallen-condition focus of that passage is in its context and background. Israel had put its trust in the security of alliances made with Assyria. Their confidence was not in God but in these treaties, and they were drunk with their own pride and self-satisfaction. The prophet is predicting destruction for them at the hand of Assyria. However, Isaiah also delivers a promise to the remnant of Israel that even in this calamitous time, the foundation for the day of the Messiah had been laid. He was encouraging the remnant of the faithful to hang on to their faith. While this was true for Israel in 730BC, the Assyrians and even Zion are, for us today, long, long ago and far, far away. However, by climbing the ladder of abstraction to talk, not of Assyrians but of attackers or opposition and temptation, and talk not just of Zion but also of hope in the promises of God, you can formulate a problem-question for the current audience.

Now that we've climbed the ladder of abstraction and paid attention to the fallen-condition focus, the problem-question for Isaiah 28:16 looks different: "What three anchors will secure us in the face of opposition?" The answers are different also, "To Christ, our atonement," "To Christ, our security," and "To Christ, our source of confidence."

Note that the Bible uses the metaphor of a stone while the problem-question uses the metaphor of a ship and an anchor. A different metaphor could be used that might be more in keeping with the text, "What three stones found our wall of defense in times of attack?" The answers would be worded very similarly, "Christ, the stone of our atonement," "Christ, the stone of our security," and "Christ, the stone of our confidence." The anchor metaphor might be more acceptable in a community where fishing, shipping, the Navy, or boating were part of the local culture. If a metaphor is implied in the text, that is preferable. However, if a secondary metaphor that helps the audience grasp the significance of God's message would be helpful, it is acceptable to choose that one.

Note the use of the first-person plural pronouns. One way to draw an audience into the problem-question is to state it in terms of those present. As Jay Adams points out, the most forceful pronoun for preaching is you. The finger is pointing at the individual in the challenge for repentance and renewal with the second-person, singular pronoun, you. The second-person plural pronoun, you is also good to use as is the first-person plural pronoun, we. Stay away from the third-person in a problem-question and in the main points of a sermon. The third-person pronoun eliminates the listener from the challenge of the text and makes the sermon about someone else. The first-person singular pronoun is equally unacceptable since it makes the sermon about the preacher.

Questions to Use

One of the criticisms of the problem-question approach has been that the question is always the same, "What does the Bible say about _____?" This need not be the case. Because of the variety of texts and the different factors influencing the audience, there should be varieties of questions - six in fact: *who, what, where, when, why, and how.* You can use each of these in some sermons. While *what* and *how* are most common, I have used them all at times. When writing a problem-question, you may compose several questions using different interrogatives. For example, the problem-question for Isaiah 28:16 could be stated using *why.* It might read, "Why is Christ our rock in crisis?" Trying these varying question statements helps to pick the most appropriate one for your audience. A good practice is to write several problem-questions for a given text using different interrogatives with possible points to answer them before selecting the best. In the appendix, read the sermon by Glenn O'Neal. Pick out the problem-question in that sermon and the points that answer it.

Frame the Answer

The text holds the answer. Go back to the text and review its main points since these will comprise the answer. Analyze the author's flow of thought to see the parts that substantiate the central point of the text. These parts become the main points that answer the sermon's problem-question. Take care in framing them.

Use the Bible's words. Using the words of the text helps the listener reference the reasons in the Bible, and it appeals to the Bible's value. When you use biblical wording during your sermon, the message seems to the listener less like human opinion and more like a message from God. Listeners will own this as their discovery of the answer as they see it in the Bible because they see the actual words. You can increase their ownership by having them visually reference the text for each main point. It is not possible to use the Bible's words all the time. You should frame the answer in terms relevant to the audience so that names such as Hagrites or places like Nineveh would be exchanged, as one climbs the ladder of abstraction, for broader generalities which apply to the current listeners. But key biblical words are worth including in these points.

It is also valuable to go in biblical order because that helps the listeners for many of the same reasons. Listeners hear what was heard in the text, and it reinforces the message. Listeners discover for themselves the author's flow of thought and tend to own it as their discovery. Using the Bible's order reduces authority issues in the small church and focuses on the text for both speaker and listener. Again it is not always possible. Sometimes the flow of thought or literary structure requires a reordering of the points in the sermon that answer the problem-question. In the Isaiah 28:16 example, the mention of a foundation and faith occur at the end of the text though they are necessarily in the first point. If you want to emphasize a view of the answer that would help the audience, it is possible to change the order of thought development in the conclusion from the biblical order. Start constructing the sermon's main points from the biblical words and order before making deviations.

Write the main points in your preaching notes as if they could answer the question. For the problem-question on Isaiah 28:16, "What three anchors will secure us in the face of opposition?" the answers all begin with, "To Christ..." The idea being conveyed is that we are anchored securely to Christ. That is the answer to the question, "We are anchored to Christ." The way we are anchored is the subject of each point.

Finally, you should state the answer in the conclusion. Restating the question throughout the course of the message helps to keep the audience on track. For example, Glenn O'Neal's sermon printed in the appendix repeats the word, "standard" or "standard of sound words" from the problem-question, "What was the 'standard of sound words' to which Paul refers which was a treasure to be guarded?" In the conclusion, you should summarize the points and state them as an answer. More will be said in the next part about developing the conclusion.

Tests of a Problem-Question Sermon

Once you write the body of the sermon consisting of the problem-question and the main points of the sermon as answers to that question, and summarize the answer, then you can test the outline. There are four primary tests for a problem-question outline: *unity, progress, diversity, balance.*[53]

Unity tests the contribution that each point makes to the whole. Each point should answer the question. It should appear as though it could stand alone in answer to the question. On the negative side of the unity test, if the point were removed, would the complete answer be impoverished? Sometimes preachers say the same thing with different words. Other times they find an insight so thrilling to them that though it does not contribute to thought of the text, it gets main point status and is not unified with the question. Look at the outline points and ask how each is unified to the problem-question.

For example, in Glenn O'Neal's sermon in the appendix, each point is a standard which Paul gives to Timothy: the minister's manner of life, the minister's attitude toward people, and the minister's presentation of the Word. Each is unified to the problem-question, "What was the 'standard of sound words' to which Paul refers which was a treasure to be guarded?"

To test the sermon's *progress* or movement, ask, "Does the point contribute in moving the sermon to a climax?" Each main point should expand and advance the knowledge of the answer to the problem that was stated in the question. If it does not, perhaps it is a rabbit trail and should be excluded.

For example, in Glenn O'Neal's sermon in the appendix, each point progresses toward a whole understanding of the standard of sound words. The points advance the sermon from the personal example of the minister to the minister's relationships to the content of the minister's communication.

The main points of a *diverse* outline say something that is exclusively different from all other points. With a half hour to fill, many preachers tend to repeat themselves in an increasingly flowery way. Repetition is a good tool, but not when used as a main point. Such redundancy will lose the audience. The *diversity* test weeds repetitions out of the main points. Remember, it is always better to say all that needs to be said in two points rather than four.

For example, in Glenn O'Neal's sample sermon each point relates a different standard for a different area of the minister's life. When added together, the standards are inclusive of the whole of the minister's life. They are his example, attitude and communication. Each one is distinct or diverse.

The *balance* test evaluates the time and material you give to each point. The sermon's the main points should be about equal to one another in time and material. If a main point is too short, then perhaps the preacher is riding a hobby horse for too long on another point. Perhaps that short point needs only more explanatory material. Or perhaps it is not a main point at all and should become a sub-point under a different main point. The *balance* test will help sort this out.

For example, Glenn O'Neal's sermon gives a picture of balance. He gives comparable space to each point.

Sermon Notes for Review

In the winter the coffee shops in rural communities begin to fill between eight and ten o'clock in the morning. The conversations over coffee vary from prices, to crops, to price supports, to news, to local sports teams. The fallen condition of mankind and their fears, sorrows, joys, and expectations do not change. The places, the names, and the numbers differ. Listening to these voices allows you to construct a sermon using the problem-question format to address the condition and the concerns of a small-church congregation. You develop the outline by answering the problem-question from the points of the biblical text. You can test the resulting outline for *unity*, *diversity*, *progress* and *balance*.

What steps will produce a problem-question outline?

1. The step from the text to the question.
2. The step from the main points of the text to the answers to the question.
3. The step to test the outline.

CHAPTER 10
TYPES OF OUTLINES

The six types of questions that require explanatory answers open the possibility of at least six types of outlines for a scriptural texts message. Yet there are even more types of problem-question outlines since the types are based on the kinds of questions and resulting explanations.[54] Some outlines derive from a kind of text that pushes the construction of both the problem-question and the outline. Other types of outlines, while consistent with the text, stress an answer that seems to suit the circumstances. Then there are outlines that give the audience direction, either stated or implied, from the outset of the problem-question. So there are three categories of outline types: outlines derived from the text, outlines stressing a kind of answer to the problem-question, and outlines that give direction to the audience response.

Outlines Derived from the Text

From an accumulation of evidence. This is an inductive process. While the entire problem-question structure for a sermon is inductive, this type of question asks for the arrangement of evidence to draw a conclusion. So the solution to the problem-question will be forensic evidence that results from the exposition of the text. When put together, that evidence will bring a conclusion.

Usually this type of outline will include the question, *How?* That question asks the evidence and its arrangement to form a conclusion. You may also formulate problem-question using *What?* although, it asks only for the listing and not the arranging of the evidence. Yet in these cases the arrangement is apparent in the order of the text.

Luke 23:27 – 35 describes Jesus' passion immediately before reaching Golgotha and being nailed to the cross. A question that asks for the accumulation and arrangement of evidence showing Jesus love for others could be, "How was the love of Christ evidenced at the cross?" The following points make the conclusion apparent:

1. He urged the women to pray for themselves.
2. He prayed for the salvation of those who placed Him on the cross.
3. He refused to save Himself in light of what He was accomplishing

From an analogy. Some outlines find a story or type in Scripture fulfilled or related in some way to our experience. These outlines are derived from an analogy with the Scripture. Sometimes the analogy is the fulfillment in the unfolding of the biblical account and the way God works with us currently. Sometimes the effects or results of a story in the Bible are analogous to the same effects for Christians today.

The question to use to making this type of outline is *How?* The question asks the text to explain how these things relate to one another. Another interrogative you can use is *What?* This word asks for a list of analogous points rather than an explanation of the analogy. An interesting interrogative to use is *Who?* Once you build the analogy from the text, then the personal application to the audience is implied in the problem-question.

Nahum 3:15 – 19 concludes Nahum's prophecy with

God's final words to the Ninevites and their king. By climbing the ladder of abstraction from Assyria and its king to nations and their leaders, the analogy becomes plain. This question asks for an analogy, "How may the final word to Assyria form God's final words to the United States?" The answers from the text are as follows:

1. God decries human strategies (vv. 15b – 17).
2. God punishes human pride (v. 18).
3. God writes the epitaph (v. 19).

From a contrast. Some outlines are derived from a contrast between two ways, two persons, two principles, etc. These two biblical sources have two different ends, rewards, or experiences. You draw lessons from the contrast between the two. On the basis of this contrast you can lay a life-change challenge before the congregants to gain the best and avoid the worst.

A problem-question outline that you derive from a contrast will most commonly lead off with *How?* The problem-question asks how these two ends are different. You may also use *What?* to begin the problem-question.

The contrast is evident in Galatians 5:16 – 26. The question would be, "What are the respective results of yielding to the flesh and the Spirit?" Here the deeds of the flesh and the fruit of the Spirit are set in contrast. There are two points in answer:

1. The flesh
2. The Spirit

The life-challenge is explicit in verse 16 and repeated in verses 25 – 26.

From an example. Biblical narratives have both heroes and rogues who present us with examples that teach about God and His work with His people. These are either negative or positive examples to either follow or stay away from. Biographies form the best material for outlines derived from examples. Paul used this approach in his writings when he told the Corinthians (1 Corinthians 10:11) that the Old Testament narratives were for an example.

Almost invariably the problem-question is formulated with *What?* The question essentially asks what the example is for us today from the given passage.

One difficult passage in Acts 5:1 – 11 relates the lies and subsequent deaths of Ananias and Sapphira. Yet it provides an example to the modern church. You can bring out this example by asking, "What realizations bring great fear to believers?" The answers are as follows:

1. We cannot serve two masters.
2. We are in a pitched battle.
3. We have the presence and work of the Holy Spirit.
4. We acknowledge accountability to the church.
5. We realize the issue of character.

From component parts of a whole. When you add the parts of the text together to complete the whole answer to the question, the outline specifies the component parts of a whole. Like a mousetrap or any piece of machinery, there are pieces that must fall into place. The machinery of the outline works as an answer to the problem-question.

To begin the problem-question that organizes the outline you'll ask *What?* and *How?* The former asks for the parts. The latter asks for the working together or interconnectedness.

Psalm two is a royal psalm to be used at the king's coronation in Israel. A sermon on the whole psalm has a problem-question, "How can you have confidence?" The answers are the components of the whole:

1. Disclaim events on earth.
2. Claim events in heaven.
3. Claim Christ.
4. Claim His ends.

From a movement in time. Some outlines come from a text that moves in a time sequence. This movement in time needs to be made clear to the audience. It is best to view this as a past, present, and future arrangement that parallels the text.

When? is the most common interrogative to begin a problem-question for a time-sequenced outline. However, you may use *Why?* and *What?* You could use *Why?* if causes or results from a past-to-present-to-future arrangement leads to the best challenge. Use *What?* if the outlined answer includes, for example, past causes, present needs and future expectations.

In Deuteronomy 8 Moses lectures Israel about the liabilities of possessing the Promised Land. He gives a remedy, but it moves in a time sequence. The question is "Why did God cause Israel to stop and think?" The answer:

1. That they might profit from the past experience.
2. That they might stress what is important in the present.
3. That they might anticipate the future in light of the power of God.

Outlines that Stress a Type of Answer

Reasoning from cause to effect. This deductive outline demonstrating reasoning from cause to effect begins with a question that asks for support for a conclusion stated or assumed in the problem-question.

The most common question used in this type of out line is *What?* The premise to be proved follows the question. You could use *How?* as the lead question. It works well when you are showing a doctrine that the biblical theology of the text explains or demonstrates.

Nahum 1:1 – 8 describes how the longtime persecutor of Israel, Assyria and its capital, Nineveh, will now be the focus of God's just judgment. The question used for this text, "Shall not the judge of all the earth deal justly?" uses a question from Genesis 18:25 as the problem-question. The *How?* is presumed in the question but left out in favor of stressing the doctrine of the justice of God. The question could be stated, "How shall the God of all the earth deal justly?" The Bible begins to develop this question with Abraham's statement about God's character when he appeals to God to spare Lot's life. Abraham assumes that God is just. This assumption is tested throughout the Old Testament to the point of Nahum's prophecy. Asaph struggled with this assumption in Psalm 73. The prophet Habakkuk struggled with it when he saw Israel's enemies prosper. Nineveh is another case where Israel's and God's enemies seem to prosper. Jonah faced the issue of Nineveh's prosperity and became angry that God, who is just, did not carry out His judgment at that time. Framing the question with Abraham's words brings the development of the biblical theology into focus. The assumption that God is a just judge is about to be proved in the case of Nineveh. So the question asks of the text how this assumption, that God is just, is proved in the case of Nineveh. The answer to the question, "Shall not the judge of all the earth deal justly?" is:

1. Yes, because of His character (vv. 1 – 3.)
2. Yes, because of His record (vv. 4 – 5.)
3. Yes, because of His rank (vv. 6 – 8.)

It should be noted that the points develop the answer according to the text.

Instruction. In outlines derived from instruction, the objective for the preacher is teaching and the objective for the congregation is learning. This is in harmony with the overall method of expository preaching. The problem-question contains words such as, "teach" or "learn." Information fills much of the content of the outline. The challenge for life-change is to learn or increase knowledge.

As a result, the singular lead interrogative is *What?* The question will ask in some form, "What do we learn?" or "What does this teach us?"

Second Corinthians 12:7 – 10 describes Paul's struggle with the thorn in his flesh. The question could be, "What does God desire to teach us about the purpose of difficult circumstances?" The answer is:

1. Be receptive to His grace (v. 9a.)
2. Be dependent on His power (v. 9b.)
3. Be content with His provision (v. 10)

Interrogation. The main points of the outline are questions in themselves. Therefore, the outline stresses interrogation.

The congregants must answer each question to get the whole answer.

In the problem-question the lead word is *What?* This is always followed by *questions*. So the essential problem-question is "What questions (if correctly answered) will ...?"

Romans 12:14 – 21 contains a series of admonitions and directives that will result in peace. The problem-question is "What seven questions will help us choose God's way?" Note that the questions derived from the text are tests for godly decision making derived from the text. The answer is as follows:

1. How am I responding?
2. With whom am I sympathizing?
3. Am I treating all the same?
4. Is it right in the sight of all?
5. Does it make for peace?
6. Do I trust God?
7. Am I overcome or over coming?

Description. Many texts in the Bible describe things. These include scenes, characteristics, history, etc. Many sermons also describe things. These include hopes, ideals, etc. One type of outline primarily stresses description. Here you may describe an event or a scene. The point is to use these descriptions to inform and shape the audience.

The most common way to begin a problem-question is to use the word *What?* You can followed this by the scene, hope, ideal, character to be described. You may also use *Where?* since many descriptions include a physical geography or a vision of heaven or hell. You can include in the *Where?* descriptions of a point of contact that is described.

Colossians 1:21 - 23 describes our position in Christ. The problem-question could be, "Where does the love of God in Christ focus?" The answer is:

1. On you as His enemy.
2. On you as reconciled in Christ.
3. On you as established in the gospel.

Outlines that Give an Audience Incentive

To follow a pattern. This is similar to an analogy, but the outline stresses progressive movement in the similarities. These outlines present a pattern to the audience. Usually an experience recorded in the Bible is compared to the experience of a person today. The defining characteristics of this type of outline are a recognizable affinity between the events of the Bible and those of people today as well as the movement of the experience from beginning to end. You then challenge the congregant to follow the pattern.

In order of frequency the interrogatives used are *What?*, *When?*, and *How?* A problem-question using *When?* emphasizes the movement over time in the similar elements. *How?* stresses the explanation of the connection between the experience in the biblical account and that of people now.

Isaiah 5:18 – 30 gives God's warning of consequences to the immoral and self-indulgent of Isaiah's day. You would draw out the parallel experience for people today by asking, "What happens when the flame of God's Word does not burn hot in God's people?" Notice that the use of *What?* and *When?* brings out the comparison of the pattern and the progression of the experience. Here is the answer from the text:

1. Coldness to God (vv. 18 – 23.)
2. The church dies (vv. 24 – 25.)
3. The nation falls (vv. 26 – 30.)

To receive an explanation. One type of outline stresses explanation with clear thinking about a text or its biblical theology as the point. It should lead the audience to think with greater clarity about the Bible, God, mankind, salvation, justification, etc. This is not just explaining about the text but rather it emphasizes the theological understandings.

Why? is the most common query. The reason is expected in the answer. That reason should then clarify the issue or doctrine. You may use *How?* to begin the problem-question. The subsequent answers show the reasoning in the explanation.

Hebrews 12:3 – 15 describes the relationship between God and those who are saved as that of a father and child. The problem-question could be "Why does God discipline His children?" Those reasons are explained from the text:

1. To demonstrate His love (vv. 3 – 9).
2. To produce the fruit of holiness (vv. 10 – 13).
3. To encourage others by our stability (vv. 14 – 15).

To accept conditions. A conditional clause always precedes the problem-question. That establishes conditions in the text that must be met to understand God's will. This kind of a sermon establishes conditions for blessing or judgment, prosperity or poverty, righteousness or sin, etc.

The most common query is *What?* But in the problem statement is the preposition, *if.* So the problem-question has a *What ... if ...?* format.

In Colossians 2:1 – 19 Paul describes how Christians are complete in Christ. They should, therefore, be immune to human judgments made by ascetic heretics from the mystery religions. A good problem-question is "What is necessary if one is to be complete in Christ?" The answers come from the text:

1. Accept His righteousness.
2. Recognize His knowledge
3. Submit to His direction

This last point is in contrast to the directions given by ascetic heretics from the mystery religions. Each point implies that the listener must meet these conditions.

To challenge to accept responsibility. Response is the aim of this type of outline. While all messages are designed for a response, this asks listeners to accept responsibility beyond the text. The challenge is implied for the audience in the problem-question and construction of the outline. Conviction and subsequent action toward a duty should result when you explain the outline.

The question is *What?* or *How?* The most common answer concerns responsibility that the individual or corporate body is expected to take. How to take on the challenge of responsibility may also be the point of the problem-question's answer. In any case the word "respond" will appear in most problem-questions under this type of outline.

In Luke 5:1 – 11 Peter responds to a miracle of Jesus while he is fishing on the Sea of Galilee. The problem-question is, "How do you respond to His call to ministry?" Using the model of Peter and the other disciples, the following outline brings the challenge:

1. Tune in … (vv. 1 – 7.)
2. Turn on … (vv. 8 – 11.)

As you preach the points of the outline you reveal the conclusions to these unfinished sentences. First, one tunes in to His call. Then one turns on His direction.

Sermon Notes for Review

The pastor of a small church was cleaning out a closet when someone came in and said he was looking for someone with a little authority. "Well, you may as well talk to me." The pastor replied. "I have as little as anyone."[55] The problem-question format helps the pastor of the small church to build the authority of the sermon on the authority of the Bible. Fourteen types of outlines use a problem-question format. There may be more yet to be tried. One or more of the six basic questions may be used to frame the problem-question: Who, what, where, when, why, and how. Each type of outline has an appropriate set of answers that make up the whole answer to the problem-question.

How would the following outlines be classified by type?

Text – Acts 14:1 – 28
Problem-Question, "What are 5 common temptations the Church faces in every age?

1. To join the political system
2. To flee pressure
3. To accept worldly adulation

4. To be shocked at the world's fickleness
5. To individualize faith

Text – Joshua 5:1 – 15
Problem-question, "Why did God bother with people, i.e. You and I?"

1. Because of a relationship of sacrifice.
2. Because of a relationship of sustenance.

Text – I Thessalonians 3:1 – 13
Problem-question, "How do you deal with discouragement?"

1. By recognizing the sources of discouragement.
2. By receiving comfort in discouragement.
3. By exercising absolute trust in God during discouragement.

SUMMARY

The problem-question format for developing a sermon outline is the best one for the small church. This format is expository in nature, faithful to the Scripture, and upholds its authority over the church. It is also best because it is consistent with the characteristics of the small church. Most importantly, it invites the audience to participate in searching the Bible to discover answers to the common concerns of life. The problem-question format levels the relationship between the preacher and the congregant, thereby making the sermon effective because of that mutual relationship. At the same time, it builds the pastor's *ethos* and credibility for effecting life-change. There are many types of outlines the expositor may use with the problem-question format.

PART 5
Delivery

Delivery of the sermon concerns all the ways that the sermon and the sermonizer connect with the audience. Obviously delivery includes the use of your voice and gestures. Yet whenever sermon development moves from being concerned about content to being concerned about the audience, we're talking about delivery. So your attitude, your view of yourself in your role, your address to, and expectations of the audience are all part of delivery. In writing the sermon, those portions that deal with the audience and that help them conceive, track, expect and act, are part of delivery. Delivery includes the introduction as well as the conclusion. You already know what you are talking about. Delivery is handing off what you have learned to a congregation for its own discovery, laughter, contrition, penance, and life-change. This part of the book emphasizes delivery practices that will fit with the characteristics of the small church.

CHAPTER 11
REMEMBERING WHO THE PREACHER IS

Ethos as we discussed already in chapter two is the credibility the preacher has with the audience. In the small church *ethos* is more important than the other two parts of the sermon, *pathos* and *logos*, because of the high value that the small church community has for relationships. The same *ethos* that the pastor has demonstrated in the web of close, face-to-face relationships that comprise the small church also affects delivery. You must have the same humble attitude while you deliver the sermon that you have for the rest of your life and ministry. It begins with the right attitudes.

Relationship to Jesus

The preacher today stands in a unique relationship to Jesus Christ. Understanding this relationship is the key to a right attitude toward yourself and your Lord. Without the right understanding and resulting attitude, preaching in the small church becomes a thankless chore and an endless losing competition with the market-driven culture in which we live.

This discouragement and doubt will speak more loudly than good exegesis or strong logic and will be communicated in the delivery. Correcting your understanding of your relationship to Jesus and His church will bring credible *ethos* in your delivery.

Moses introduced the Mosaic covenant and the Law that governed Israel. Along with the Law he instituted the offices of king, priest, and prophet to administer its requirements (Deuteronomy 17:14; 18:1, 15.) The prophets were God's preachers in Israel. Whether they wrote or not, they were first and foremost preachers who spoke on behalf of God. In Deuteronomy 18:18, God promises the Israelites that the prophets would speak on His behalf. But in the same passage He specifies that they must never exceed the standard of Moses' teachings. Some of them wrote down their prophecies, but far more of them only spoke. They explained, applied, exhorted and rebuked based on the authority of Moses. They even told, with long-range foresight the outcomes of obedience and disobedience.

In like manner, the preacher today stands in relationship to the Lord Jesus Christ who is the mediator of the New Covenant. On more than one occasion, Jesus claimed to have supplanted Moses (John 5:43 – 47.) Like Moses, Jesus spoke as the seminal lawgiver of the New Covenant. His words would be the test stone and standard for all who followed in that covenant (John 12:48 – 49.) Just as the prophets of the Old Testament were preachers of the Mosaic covenant and the Law that embodied it so the preacher of the New Covenant is to preach Jesus and His Word to His church. The writing apostles in the New Testament expounded and explained Jesus and His will in order to take the church through the present age to the Second Advent. The sacred task of the preacher is to expound and explain to the church in every generation the person, word and will of Jesus. This is in accordance with the understanding of 2 Timothy 4:2 (see chapter 6.) Jesus our Lord intends His preachers to carry out His sacred calling and task for His church.

The Lord Jesus creates the church. Preaching does not. The Lord Jesus Christ has revealed sufficient content to take His church through the good-to-evil vicissitudes of each succeeding generation until He Himself comes for His church. The preacher lacks nothing in order to faithfully and humbly serve the church. You have no greater object than the church the Lord has created. You have no more to offer than what the Lord has given in His Word.

While the size of the church may affect the manner of address in some ways, the role of preaching is no less important for the small church. The preacher remains the same herald and prophet of the Lord Jesus Christ to His church in any size congregation. Jesus has called the small church into existence. He will feed and nourish His church through the preaching of His Word whether small or large.

You come to your task as the divine representative of the Lord Jesus Christ. The pulpit in the small church or the large church is the same size, for it represents the same Lord. You can come to your sermon with the assurance that whether your preaching draws a small congregation or a large one, the greatness and importance of your task comes from the approval and blessing of the Lord.

Before you speak a word of the sermon, you approach your congregation as a servant. You serve whatever the Lord has ordered for their nourishment. You do not make this food that the spirit of each congregant needs. You only deliver it. You make it palatable and digestible by making the ancient text intelligible and actionable. The Holy Spirit will apply the nourishment of the Word in a life-changing way to each member of the congregation. You approach the congregation with humility. You become meek and self-effacing before the congregation, knowing that your influence for life-change comes only from your faithfulness to the Lord and His Word and from the work of the Holy Spirit.

Your *ethos* comes from your confidence in the Christ-ordained task and your humility as a servant of the congregation. These attitudes are the beginning of delivery. Your attitudes of a willing, humble, and faithful servant create a winning *ethos* in a small church.

Hearing the voice of God

While a preacher was writing a sermon, his little son watched. The son said, "Daddy, does the Lord tell you what to say?"

"Of course He does." answered his father.

"Then," came back the boy, "why do you keep scratching some of it out?"[56]

The steps, exercises, and processes that go into writing a sermon seem far removed from the sermon's theology. The sermon should somehow represent the voice of God. Through all your efforts to prepare a sermon you need to hear that voice and communicate it. Without a sense of having heard the voice of God, without the anticipation that the audience will hear the voice of God, your delivery of the sermon is just another effort.

The sermon's delivery is based on your research into the text. As academic as that research must be, it is also a spiritual exercise. Through the exegesis of the text you step away from the contemporary context and into the context of the initial preaching and hearing of the Bible's message. You hear the intent of God in delivering a message to the people of that historical time and that geographical place. You try to step behind the static wall of translations to hear the fluid stream of communication between God and His people. Exegesis is meditating on the text so you can listen to the intonation, connotation, and expression that accompany the divine dialogue. In addition you attempt to stand in the sandals of those who first heard the message. You want to measure the weight of the burden of this interaction with God. You share their concerns, fears, expectations, and hopes. In this spiritual exercise you hear the voice of God.

This difficult spiritual journey is complicated by the brevity of the time you have to explore and experience God's Word. In only six days you must deliver another sermon. Other preparations must receive the same investment in that same period of time. Add to these all the concerns of a small-church pastor, and the difficulty is compounded. But if you take the journey intentionally, seriously, and prayerfully, the experience of hearing the voice of God grips you before you decide on any points of the message. Being gripped by God's message to His people in the Bible profoundly shapes your delivery.

Sermon development requires another hearing of the voice of God. Once you have studied the text and understand the message of God to His people, then you can write the sermon. As you take the main point of the text and state it in the form of a problem-question, you listen a second time to the voice of God. You stand in the shoes of the congregation to hear in God's voice the message for the people today. The message cannot be about what people want to hear. It cannot be about what you want to say to them. The sermon is what God wants to say to them. Having immersed yourself in the message of God to His people, you listen again for the message of God to *this* people on *this* coming Sunday. Through this process, your confidence grows that the sermon you'll deliver is God's message and not yours.

You express this confidence in the delivery. Having confidence that the sermon is God's voice to his people frees you in delivery. The success of your sermon does not depend on eloquence or logic but on the power of the voice of God (Psalm 29:4 – 5.) You are giving away the very power that has gripped you in study and directed you in writing the sermon. The sermon is not something that accrues to your honor, but it becomes a blessing that you freely give. The power of the Word, applied by the Holy Spirit as you have experienced it, will "break the cedars" (Psalm 29:5) of people's will and effect life-change. D. Martyn Lloyd-Jones said:

> This element of freedom is all important. Preaching should be always under the Spirit – His power and control – and you do not know what is going to happen. So always be free. It may sound contradictory to say "prepare, and prepare carefully", and yet "be free." But there is no contradiction ... You will find that the Spirit Who has helped you in your preparation may now help you, while you are speaking, in an entirely new way, and open things out to you which you had not seen while you were preparing.[57]

This confidence and resulting freedom lead to a sense of anticipation that you and the audience will hear from God in powerful ways.

Contract with the audience

A well-known Irish preacher began to bellow to a packed audience of about 400 without the aid of a microphone from the strength of a strong, well developed diaphragm, "My brrr-rothers, in the Bible..." As I listened he had laid out the terms of our relationship for the rest of the sermon. He would dominate us by the force of his voice, and we would sit and listen in subdued silence except for a polite laugh at his humor because of the authoritative use of the Bible. This was a contract with the audience. This contract was set in the sermon's introduction. The introduction is critical because it forms a contract with the audience about the relationship it has with the preacher for the remainder of the sermon. Among small-church goers this contract places the sermon in the context of the church body's relationships. Their acceptance of the message and participation in it hinge on this contract.

The first goal of an introduction is lowering negative relationship barriers. You face aggressive relationship barriers when you step into the pulpit. Some of these may be hostility. Some people may be at church but are upset by an issue or conflict outside the worship context. Something preceding the sermon such as distasteful music or someone else's comments or behavior, may have upset some listeners. Less aggressive but just as distracting are all the personal disturbances such as financial worries or family difficulties or personal fears that make listeners dread the time they must give to sitting quiet while the minister "drones on." Passive but negative barriers that you must address in the introduction include confrontational issues. While listeners may not easily get up and walk out, they do not have the means to direct the conversation nor change the channel. They must accept an unfavorable balance of authority in the communication pattern with you being in the authoritative position while they are in a submissive position. Your introduction must draw people from those things that aggressively distract them from listening as well as overcome the passive communication barriers that arise.

To overcome these barriers, create a contract with the audience in the introduction. Prayer overcomes barriers to listening. Asking the audience to join in prayer puts both preacher and listener in place of submission to God. Prayer is essential, for you must be submissive to God as you deliver the sermon. Prayer also lifts both you and the listener out of the grasp of distracting irritations, struggles, or fears.

When you express appreciation for the opportunity to speak, it relieves confrontational barriers. Appreciation gives back to the listeners some of the power during the sermon's interaction because you recognize their gift of time and attention that you depend upon.

Humor or light heartedness will, also lower barriers to communication. Victor Borge put it this way, "Laughter is the shortest distance between two people." Laughter is mutual. Sadness, seriousness, or intensity is not mutual because different people experience each emotion at differing levels. Commenting about the weather or the circumstances of the time or setting or planning humor in the formal introductory material will shorten the emotional distance between you and the listener. In the small church, this is even more necessary.

The small-church congregation needs to know that you are coming from the same context as they are and not from an academic ivory tower or a metaphysical cloud. Your introduction makes a contract with the audience to bring your sermon's content into that mutual context. The small-church context is usually the same for all your listeners. The relationships of the small church and its surrounding community that you are immersed in will have a culture of humor and a great deal of news and stories you can use for these light hearted comments. The ability to laugh at ourselves is the first step to conviction and repentance. While it is always bad for you to minimize or denigrate what you are about to do, you should use the introduction to create the best environment for active, participatory listening.

The introduction should be "inciteful." It should incite the audience to take interest in the sermon because you need the audience to be favorable toward the sermon and its content. You should also induce the audience to anticipate the vitality of the message for themselves. Your introduction should always seek to pique the interest in the text that you will expound. Humor encourages interest. The humor you use in the introduction should not be a series of humorous but unrelated anecdotes.[58] Rather you can open the thinking of the audience to the sermon by choosing the right stories. If you can humbly use yourself as an example of someone this passage speaks to, you will win the interest of the small-church audience.

In a recent sermon I revealed in the introduction my own struggle with "prayer guilt." The audience began to smile and nod to acknowledge their similar experience. This led the way to my sermon on prayer from John 17. To begin an exposition of Isaiah 10 delivered on July 4, 2004 this author contrasted the terror attacks in Spain with the last line of the U. S. Declaration of Independence to incite audience interest in the text.

Use a variety of techniques to incite your audience to desire an answer to the coming problem-question. Each part of the introduction, appreciation, prayer, humor, story, statistic, or other means should lead the listeners to desire an answer to the problem-question. For example, the introduction about the experience of "prayer guilt" led the audience to want to know "What is on the Jesus' prayer list?" according to John 17. Or the contrast between the terrorist attack in Spain and the last line of the Declaration of Independence led the audience to want to know "Who makes the world go round?" according to Isaiah 10. You should measure the potential of your introduction to incite the audience to probe God's Word with you for answers to the problem-question.

The introduction should be "inciteful" in two ways. It should positively dispose the audience to listen. Second, the introduction should raise the audience's level of anticipation for the problem-question and its answer. For these reasons it is often best to complete the sermon outline, including the conclusion of the sermon before you craft the introduction. Using this order you can write an introduction with the best material and even the best wording to incite the audience to listen.

The introduction should also be "insightful." Tie the introduction to the theme of the text. As you study a narrative passage of Scripture, you should always ask yourself, "Where does this happen in the lives of the people here and now?" Or in the case of a teaching passage, you should ask, "Where does this word from God naturally interject itself into the life experiences of people here and now?" Small-church pastors who are involved in the daily lives of their people can see this more readily. As you prepare the introduction, you are in the position to select a bit of humor or an anecdote or statistic that has the peculiar smack of reality for your hearers.

When this author was a new pastor in wheat-farming country, one of the farmers in the church pointed out the lesson of "cheat" grass. I had the opportunity to use that in connection with the parable of the wheat and the tares. Of course the congregation already knew the analogy, but they had a heightened interest in the message and I was united with them in the search for God's message in the parable. Use surprise as much as possible to lure your audience into the Bible's answer to their needs. When your listeners learn surprise insights that connect the text with the introduction, it heightens their interest level in finding the answer to the problem-question. Use a connecting sentence for a narrative passage such as, "That is the way it must have been in the case of these guys in the Bible." This makes the surprise connection between some local story or bit of humor and the ancient text you are expounding. Good introductions set up the legitimacy of the problem-question. Because of the introductory story or anecdote you have raised a problem, but you have not articulated it in the introduction. When you state the problem-question, the problem from the introduction is already legitimate. Now you have conceptualized and articulated the problem in a question form so the Bible text becomes the necessary place to search for that answer.

Servant to the audience

Your objective in serving the sermon to the audience is the delivery. It is like presentation in cooking. When the meal is served, you see the steam rising or the color and arrangement of the food. You smell the aromas of the dishes and their spices and relishes. You may even hear the sizzle of a hot plate or the crunch of lettuce. All these direct your appetite to the taste of the food. Sermon delivery stimulates the audience to take in the spiritual nourishment of the Word of God that you expound. So sermon portions such as the conclusion and the transitions serve the audience in the course of the sermon.

Transitions are the statements you make between the main points of the sermon. The transition between each point serves the audience in three ways. First a transition *wraps up* the previous point for the listener. It also may *rap up* the previous point to affect the listener. A transition then *ramps up* to the next point for the listener.

Analyze, explain, define, illustrate, and rephrase the material in each sub point. The transition *wraps* this detail up into a restatement of the previous main point as proven. The transition always serves as a summary of what has been discovered. This helps the audience to track the logic and understand that the argument is complete at this point.

If a quote, statistic, anecdote, proverb or personal confession can add weight to the summary, then the transition can *rap* up your previous point in that way. By these or other techniques, the *pathos* of the audience is *rapped* and increased to make a lasting impression. A couple of cautions are in order. It is not always possible to do this. First, too much illustrative material can be distracting from the point being driven home. The point you want to drive home could be overshadowed by a dramatic *rap-up* story. The right things are hard to find for every point so be prudent about what *rap- up* material you use in the sermon.

The transition should *ramp-up* the audience's anticipation of the next point as part of the whole answer. When you follow your summary, perhaps by something such as a hard hitting bit of illustration, it brings the audience to a statement concerning what is to come. This may be as simple as the phrase, "...which leads us too..." Or one may say, "Having grasped this, you won't understand the whole answer (to the problem-question) without..." Such statements ramp the audience up to get the next point.

Hopefully, the sermon sends the congregation out to grow in their spiritual lives and their witness because they have been fed from the Word of God. The sermon's conclusion should facilitate that growth. Too often the conclusion is such a vague afterthought that the diverse members of the audience may come up with their own creative applications. You better serve the audience when the sermon *comes together* and *goes out* through a well-planned conclusion. The audience *comes together* around the answer to the problem-question. The sermon's points come together as a whole in the conclusion. You have exposed the answer to the problem-question piece by piece from the text. Now the conclusion needs some kind of whole statement of the answer to the problem. Review those pieces to see the overall connection. Now sum up the whole for the listener in a clear statement of the answer. Through the summary of the main points and the statement of the answer to the problem-question the audience, comes together in one mind about the Bible's answer to the problem-question.

In the conclusion you should restate this answer as God's will for the audience. The people of God will not carry out the Bible's admonitions and directives if they believe that they are the optional opinions of the preacher. But given the presence and ministry of the Holy Spirit, God's people will come to a common agreement about God's will for their lives. They *come together*.

Through the sermon's conclusion, the congregation also *goes out*. One way to send the congregation out to intentionally fulfill and live out what they have heard is to use an illustration. While it is not always necessary, a story that visualizes the carrying out of the will of God can motivate listeners to attempt to do what the Bible says. The illustration should provoke the emotion of hope for a better or more fruitful life for those who will attempt to carry out God's will. A second way to send the listeners out is by giving them specific prescriptions for implementation. The congregation needs to be able to act upon the sermon's conclusion. Even though not every member of the congregation will have an opportunity to act upon the prescribed activities, they will still see those activities as commendable and that they should be part of the congregation's culture and ethic. At the end of a recent sermon on Mother's Day the conclusion posed a problem in making it applicable to all the listeners. The text was 2 Timothy 1:5 and 3:14 – 15. The problem-question was, "What can a mother do?" The answer had two points: give and teach. I concluded with a humorous story of a failing on my own mother's part. Then

I emphasized that while we are not all mothers, and those who are, aren't perfect, we can all appreciate, value, pursue, applaud and imitate mothers who do teach and give to their children.

Sermon notes for review

When I helped a farmer with the silage harvest, I was responsible to drive the dump-truck and dump the harvest into a silage pit. Because I'd never driven a dump-truck before, I was given brief instructions on the mechanics of dumping silage. I backed up to the pit, set the brake, and lifted the dump handle. The load shifted to the dump gate and began to slide into the pit. At the same time, the front of the truck began to lift off the ground. Soon the silage, the truck, and I would all be upside down in the pit. Quickly lowering the dump handle the load shifted back to the front. What a relief! I should have lifted the dump handle a little at a time, so the silage slipped slowly into the pit, while I remained safely above with the truck. In the same way a sermon needs to be delivered, not dumped. Effective delivery begins before the sermon. The sermon in a small church is not an exercise in public speaking. It is a live relationship acted out in the course of the sermon between the preacher, God, and the congregation. The delivery begins with your journey through study. You must hear the voice of God. That will result in both confidence as you preach and freedom to speak as the Holy Spirit does His work. Delivery is always set in a contract between you and the audience. The introduction should set that contract in the small church in such a way that it is relationship-based and invites participation in a journey of mutual discovery from the Bible. The introduction should lead to the body of the sermon by being both "inciteful" and "insightful." The preacher is a servant to the church of Jesus Christ. The pastor is a servant of the congregation through delivery. Transitions between points serve to track the audience's understanding with the development of the sermon. Transitions *wrap up* the previous point. They may *rap up* the audience's emotional conviction about that point. They also *ramp up* to the next point. Conclusions serve the audience as well. A well-planned conclusion causes the audience to *come together* in one mind about God's will and to *go out* in an effort to act on what the Bible has said.

How can a preacher serve the small church congregation?

1. By the right attitude
2. By the best contract in the introduction
3. By service in the transitions
4. By calling the congregation together and sending them out with the conclusion

CHAPTER 12
RHETORICAL DELIVERY

As the pastor finished up a sermon on the majesty, greatness and immense value of God, he contrasted our humble unworthiness with God's presence. In sacred quietness he uttered the closing prayer. Beseeching God to remind the congregation of their humble state, he said, "...for we are, Lord, but dust." Only in some haste to bring the service to a close he gave emphasis to the wrong word. The elder's wife thought to herself, "Oh my! Did our pastor just call us all 'butt dust'?" In her startled state, she felt the pew begin to shake violently. Alarmed she popped open one eye to see her husband, the Elder, manfully attempt to stifle a guffaw. How we say things makes a difference. Delivery is planning how to say things.

Extemporaneous Delivery

Small churches live by their stories. These stories form their identity more than sociological factors or the vision of the leadership. The story above comes from a small church where the pastor has served for over twenty-five years. It has been retold many times and will continue to be retold for years to come. This example of a small church confirms the oral nature of the small church. This oral nature affects the sermon's delivery. Extemporaneous delivery allows maximum freedom for how you say things. You must conduct a live conversation between God in His Word, and the congregation of the small church.

First the Bible is oral, and most of it is narrative. Israelites told these stories orally to one another and to succeeding generations. Oral delivery of the sermon fits with the small church and with the Bible. In recent times, the use of varied media as part of the sermon has caused many to despise the value of this oral relationship. Even in small churches, the presence of the digital projector has become common. This has been driven by the need to have music inexpensively available for congregational singing. One refurbished digital projector costs less than an entire set of new hymnals, and the range of music available to project is almost inexhaustible. As a result the pressure develops on the small-church preacher to use PowerPoint presentations in place of oral sermons. While it may seem to be an efficient use of this newly available tool, two negative results are turning off more and more projectors in small churches.

First the pastor's contract with the audience is substantially altered when one changes from strictly oral communication to PowerPoint. The sanctuary becomes a lecture hall, the sermon is the plenary lecture in a Sunday conference on spiritual life, and you present yourself as the expert on the business of spiritual life. You demonstrate this by your professional-looking PowerPoint presentation.

A second negative result is that PowerPoint instead of a sermon diminishes the power of the Bible. It reduces the Bible's narrative down to a set of outlined propositions. The congregation is expected to master these propositions for the implied test after the service rather than be gripped by the power of the story of the God's work with His people. Not only does this diminish the narrative portions of the Bible, but it also removes the personal quality of the didactic letters. New Testament letters reveal passion and compassion from the heart of an apostolic missionary and pastor to his flock. With PowerPoint they can be reduced to mere clip art minimizing their oral message.

In a small church it is better not to use the projector regularly since it diminishes the *ethos* of the pastor and the quality of the relationship between the preacher and the congregation. Even movie clips should be used sparingly. Those in small churches often live in poor areas that are not the focus of Hollywood glamour. The video clip seems to reinforce that fact and tell the small-church group that real drama and significant life events happen elsewhere. This diminishes the *pathos* of the sermon which results from your real life relationship to your congregation. The *pathos* of the movie grips the audience and not the Bible as related through the pastor. One rural church made good use of a video clip when the pastor and some people in the church created a brief vignette using a hand-held camera that made a point. It worked because it involved familiar settings and people that the congregation knew. So, though contrived, it was one of their stories.

At the heart of the extemporaneous sermon is your conversation with your congregation about the Bible and its message. In the sermon you tie together the story of the community and of the Bible. Jay Leno used to take the first ten minutes of the *Tonight Show* to talk about current events. He would poke fun, point out foibles and reveal ironies. He did this for a community, his television audience. Educated, middle and upper-middle class people from urban areas were the members of that community. You do the same for your small-church community - hopefully with far less crass irreverence. You can talk about not only the humorous but also the joyous and the distressing events of community life. You do this not to flatter the audience but to connect their narrative to that of the Bible. In one church I pastored, a husband and wife were leading the singing when she blanched and nearly fainted. Someone caught her. An ambulance took her to the hospital. We had all just learned that she was pregnant with their second child.

As I stepped to the pulpit there, I saw a pool of blood on the floor where she had been standing. It seemed to be evidence of our worst fears for her pregnancy. We prayed fervently. I gave the sermon but not as planned. The story of the life of the community had radically changed. However, the next week, our grief, fear, and anxiety were replaced with joy and celebration when it was announced that Mom and baby were healthy and out of any danger. Again the sermon I gave was different than planned because the story of the community had taken another turn. The pastor is in constant conversation throughout the week with the community of faith and with the broader community. The sermon is the verbal expression of that conversation, and, as such, ought always to be extemporaneous.

Extemporaneity describes the delivery style. If you are in a conversation with the congregation of the small church, then conversational tone is your base delivery style. Yelling is rarely ever a part of that style. Conversational style does not include affected diction that communicates a higher culture than the community's. Learning to speak in the vocabulary and diction of the community of the small church will win you approval. Preaching conversationally limits the use of force in your voice that drives the sound through the sinuses. This affected stained-glass tone is unnatural and not conversational. Conversation is not forced in diction or tone but begins lower in the voice box and without stress.

Glenn O'Neal said, "Speak in a conversational manner but with intensity."[59] While a conversation may not be loud, it is often intense. Intensity is the way that people in conversation express enthusiasm, anxiety and conviction. In conversation an intense speaker may speed up with enthusiasm, or slow down to illustrate fear, or drop to a husky voice with the emotion of conviction. None of these are off-putting but draw the small-church congregant into the conversation as if between two people and not as a lecture about an important subject. Conversation often has pauses. A pause will draw the audience to look at you to study your body language and facial expression to better understand what you are preaching. A pause is more effective in a small church where the space between you and the audience is more personal. Conversational tone builds on the preacher/parishioner relationship.

Extemporaneity also means the freedom to speak. That freedom is guarded by the way that you prepare your notes. Some preachers write a manuscript and read so they don't have to be concerned about the sermon content being misrepresented. Others memorize a sermon and deliver it without referring to anything except the Bible so they can be free to have eye-contact with the audience. These two extremes will not give you the freedom you need for a small-church congregation. While both are good practices at times, the former changes the quality of the communication from a conversation to an essay. The emphasis of an essay is to communicate with correct literary form rather than have a personal conversation. Memorization consumes the preacher with the burden of recall. The preacher who memorizes becomes the actor who is reciting and performing. The best form of preparation is to use an outline. You can write out portions such as introductions, illustrations and conclusions because prescribed wording is important for effective delivery. But when you put the content in outline form, you can move through key points while remaining free to maintain personal contact with the audience, select the proper phrasing, and use repetition as your relationship to the audience seems to require. John Broadus recommended this type of extemporaneous preaching:

> By natural extension the phrase 'extemporaneous speaking' is applied to the cases in which there has been preparation of thought, however thorough, but the language is left to be suggested at the moment. Still further, when notes are made, as a help to preparation, when the plan of the discourse is drawn out on paper, and all the principal points are stated or suggested, we call it extemporaneous speaking, because all this is

regarded only as a means of arranging the recalling the thoughts, and the language is extemporized.[60]

When you use outline notes, it frees your language for the moment but keeps the thoughts tied to the exposition. It brings the balance between relationship and authority to preaching in the small church.

Always while preaching, Russ Richardson carries a big Bible open in his hand. When referencing the text, he puts his finger on the verses to direct audience attention there. Few preachers appear to be more directly and literally biblical in their delivery. What the audience cannot see, are the Post-it notes that line the margins of his Bible. These track his thoughts with the exposition of the text while he relates to his small congregation in a personal and friendly manner.

Techniques for Focusing Attention

Intonation helps people focus their attention. Television and other mass communication have reduced the number of regional accents along with their distinctiveness. At the same time the voice intonation that speakers on television use has become the standard for public speaking. By contrast, flat, unemotional speech has become a form of comedy that Ben Stein has used to make a lot of money. The rise and fall of a voice's volume and pitch are normal to the ear and can be easily imitated. Voice patterns that imitate meaning are another use of intonation. "Aaalll theeee waaayyyeee!" emphasizes the meaning of the phrase. Slurring the pitch up can emphasize the question. Staccato speech may emphasize a point, "Turn...to...God...to...day!" Listen to media announcers and practice imitating their voice patterns.

Several other techniques focus audience attention. Incorrect readings of quotes from the Bible or other well-known sources can focus attention. If you wrote a conflation (see chapter 3) of a passage you can use it to focus attention on the text or the point of the sermon. With a problem-question format, be careful of using questions to focus attention since there is already one on the table - the problem-question. Listeners may become confused about which question the sermon is trying to answer. However, asking questions of the audience can be helpful. For example, "What do you think when...?" In the small church these need not be rhetorical, but you may expect an answer to focus attention on the sermon. You can introduce a supposition that would be contrary to the meaning of the text. This will highlight the text's meaning.

Illustrating the sermon is another way that you bring attention to the meaning of the text. Three ways of illustrating the sermon are important when preaching in the small church. They are cross references, metaphor, and story.

Cross references to Bible passages other than the text you are expounding are illustrative rather than part of the content. Cross references have an added value for use with the problem-question outline because they enhance the audience's sense of discovery. Taking a small-church audience to a cross reference heightens the sense of participation. O'Neal breaks the use of cross references into three kinds: explanatory, supplementary and confirmatory.[61] The first use of a cross reference explains a meaning in the text that is perhaps not as readily grasped. One way to give an explanation to the audience is to point out the connection between the two passages when you cite the cross reference. For example, the same word or phrase used by the same author in a different context will illuminate the use in the context you are studying. John the Baptist's declaration of Jesus the Lamb of God (John 1:29) provides explanation for the image of the lamb in Revelation 5:6. You can also tell a story behind the cross reference. Matthew ties the advent of Jesus to the Old Testament types by using quotations. The emotional impact of the quote from Micah 5:2 in Matthew 2:6 can be explained by telling the story of the Assyrian invasion and God's deliverance in Micah's day. You would lay out these connections as an explanation of the text.

Cross references can also supply added detail to the expounded text. When Paul says in Romans 13:8 "Owe nothing to anyone except to love one another..." you can turn to 1 Corinthians 13 to supplement the nature and extent of the debt of love. While being careful not to turn from an exposition of Romans to an exposition of 1 Corinthians, lay out just enough detail to give practical insights about what the obligation to love might look like in terms of attitudes and actions. This kind of supplementary material in the body of the sermon sets up a challenge to life-change in the conclusion.

Biblical writers repeat themes and key words. The entire Bible contains repeated themes and types. When you cite these repetitions outside the text being expounded, it confirms the point you made about the text. In expounding 1 Peter 5, confirm the point Peter is making by reviewing the type of shepherd and sheep found in the Psalms and Jesus' teaching. This is the confirmatory use of cross references.

Even though it is very simple and subtle, a metaphor grabs the audience by making implicit comparisons with the common experiences of life. Psalm 91:4 tells us that God offers wings to take refuge under. The metaphor is of the hen protecting her chicks. The hen is the image of succor, nurture, and protection. Jesus picks up on this image in Luke 13:34 where he speaks of God's protection as being like that of a hen protecting her young. All who heard the Psalms or heard Jesus would have seen a hen offering her wings to her chicks. They would have understood the metaphor. The preacher needs to find metaphors from life that illustrate truth and touch the audience's storehouse of common experiences. For example, wrinkles provide a metaphor that people today would be able to visualize. The metaphor of how clothing gets wrinkles through neglect and inattention and how they are removed by a hot iron can provide an illustration of sin, rebuke and correction for many passages. You can do it in a few words that will grip the audience and provide a future connection to the passage as they encounter wrinkles in daily experience. Metaphors can come from family life, personal hygiene, employment, driving, finances, sports, media, etc. I used braking as a metaphor in a sermon. I had driven a grain truck for a farmer during harvest. In a frightening near-accident I discovered that the braking distance of a loaded truck is much greater than the braking distance of an empty truck. This provided a metaphor for the effect of carrying a load of un-confessed sin. A great resource for finding the metaphors in the Bible is the *Dictionary of Biblical Imagery*.[62]

Reportedly, Ernest Hemingway was challenged to tell a story in six words. He came back with, "For sale: baby shoes, never worn."[63] Story can have a great impact when told with such force. While much is written about storytelling in sermons, the preacher in the small church should make one important consideration. Since stories are part of the church's identity, in most small congregations these stories will be told over and over. You will do well to build your credibility with the small congregation by telling these stories in the course of your preaching as the opportunity allows. You must tell the story so that it serves the sermon and illustrates God's message to His people rather than merely flattering the congregation. Craft the story to bring the point home. Like Hemingway's story, your story must build tension and then come to resolution. That resolution can be tragic like Hemmingway's or comic like my story of braking distances of loaded trucks. That resolution should make your point in the sermon. A good story is worth telling if the point in the plot's resolution brings home the point that is being made from the text. You can bring the point home with emotion, whether that emotion is laughter, joy, fear, or grief. The emotion should be concurrent with the emotion generated by the biblical text. The point should be obvious and require little explanation on your part to make the connection. A simple phrase such as, "In the same way..." or "We should feel the same..." will suffice to make the connection. Abstract connections will require too much explanation.

Sermon Notes for Review

One preacher was called back to a former church. He

asked one of the deacons why, "We didn't want no preacher nohow," the deacon responded, "and you were the nearest to no preacher we could get."[64] Sometimes being less of a preacher is best. In the small church being less preacherly and more extemporaneous is best. The effectiveness of the extemporaneous sermon in the small church is threatened by the use of media, because it changes the contract with the audience and moves the motive of the sermon to professional media and off the relationship of preacher and congregation. Extemporaneous delivery means to tell the story of the Bible and connect it with the story of the faith community as experienced in the events of daily life. You must be free to respond and interact with that community life and history in the sermon. Extemporaneity is maintained in delivery by preaching from a set of outline notes. Outline notes free the wording and eye-contact but tie the thought development to the exposition. Use a variety of techniques to draw attention to the sermon. Those requiring the most planning are cross references, metaphor, and story.

How do you tell a sermon?

1. Extemporaneously
2. Illustratively

CHAPTER 13
PERFORMANCE OF DELIVERY

Old television sitcoms filmed before live studio audiences had an element of scripting. The actors had lines and movements to deliver to the audience. But these were subsidiary to a performance delivery that was interactive with the studio audience. Sermon delivery has to do with the words that are crafted for the audience. That is the rhetorical delivery described in the previous chapter. Sermon delivery also has to do with the performance of the sermon. Certainly no preacher wants to be considered just a performer. Yet in the small church, because a real-time interactive relationship dominates the sermon, performance as part of delivery must be considered in the process of preaching.

Attitude Matters in Delivery

As stated in chapter eleven, your attitude results from your relationship with God. You must have heard from God in the study of the text so that the message has meaning in the context of your own life and ministry. You must have also heard from God as the congregation's representative. In this way it is God's message to His people and not your message. Both your study and what you've heard from God give you an attitude of confidence. Rightly founded, this attitude avoids two common pitfalls - pride and feelings of superiority on one hand and self-deprecation on the other. You will not speak down to your congregation but you will talk with them. You will not use bombast to carry your argument. A new preacher was setting up his office at a small church when he found the previous preacher's sermon notes. In the margin of one sermon he saw in red, "Yell like blazes! Point weak."[65] On the other hand, that preacher won't diminish the authority of what is being preached saying, "But then again, what do I know?" "Thus saith the Lord" forms the unspoken presupposition of every sermon. You must approach the sermon with the confidence that you are God's agent to communicate His message. You do not manipulate the audience but neither do you step back from legitimate rebuke or open challenge.

On one occasion I was invited to come from our rural community to a nearby small town and lead a brief segment on the radio. The experienced and professional radio announcers always projected a positive and upbeat attitude to the listeners. When I watched them, I saw why. They smiled into the microphone. They told me that when you smile, even though no one sees your face, your voice changes appropriately. Smiling will make the message more engrossing to the congregation, so begin with a smile. Talk with a smile as the sermon progresses. Certainly serious subjects need sterner faces, but the base should be a smile. Reportedly, Spurgeon was once told his student preachers, "When you preach on heaven let your face radiate the joy and glory of God. When you preach on hell your regular face will do." Make the effort to smile. The rest will take care of itself.

Someone described evangelist Sam Jones as preaching with his head down. "...as if he was holding on to his chain of thought by the teeth."[66] Another nonverbal technique that keeps one from looking completely bound in one's chain of thought is raised eyebrows. The seriousness of the task, the feverish effort to keep the content clear and maintain theological integrity can cause knitted brows and pinched expressions. Slightly raising your eyebrows communicates a positive expectation. This will be contagious to the audience. Such a simple technique enhances your preaching in the small church because your audience can see your expressions and is in the habit of reading them in other circumstances. Practicing, even in front of a mirror, makes smiling and raised eyebrows more natural.

Action Carries the Message

Approach sermon time with expectation. When the time comes, move energetically to the pulpit. Smile as described above. These actions suggest that something good is about to happen. The audience begins to raise its expectations that the result of the sermon time will be both helpful and hopeful. They perceive that you are ready and eager and will read this as a sign that God has spoken to you and you are prepared.

Move with the sermon. It is best to leave the pulpit once you are in the process of speaking. The sacred desk has its rightful place and deserves respect from the congregation. But it does not restrict your movement. In the small church movement enhances personal conversational style. At a time of casual information or story telling, it is appropriate to lean on the pulpit casually. Step away altogether for whole-body movements that enact the text of the Bible or your illustrating story. This move-away from the pulpit is even more necessary if the audience is seated widely across the room rather than narrowly down the length of the room. Stepping away allows for equal close contact with the congregation on all sides of the pulpit. In the pulpit, lean forward for intensity. Step back to demonstrate fear or speak with extra volume.

Move with the audience as well as with the sermon. Get your directions correct. North should be pointed to accurately.

Left and right should be their left and right and not yours. It is confusing if they see the goats on the left as being on their right (Matthew 25:41.) When making reference to the cross, point to the cross. Point to the communion table or in the direction of heaven or hell, when these are your subjects. Auditory helps are also part of the communication. Don't hesitate to make noises appropriate to the text. Many narrative portions have sounds that you can reasonably expect would have accompanied the story. During a sermon on Luke 10:38ff, I made the sounds that would have accompanied Martha as she worked in the kitchen while resenting Mary who sat quietly at Jesus' feet. While I described pots being set down and picked up and cupboard doors violently opened and closed all as Mary sat quietly, I also used my hand on the pulpit surface to make the sound of heavy stomping across the kitchen floor that would have communicated Martha's envy. I hadn't realized the effect until visiting with a shut-in woman who had heard the sermon on tape. The story had come alive for her through the sound-effects. Walk across the platform when walking with the Lord. Pull imaginary ropes to set the cross up in place. Move with the sermon.

Audience Contact is Important

The most obvious form of contact is eye-contact. Look squarely into their faces. You'll learn the audience reaction by this effort. When their interest is flagging you will see it and adjust. When faces become quizzical, your extra repetition or explanation will help. Eye-contact has value for the congregation. While there is risk that someone in the congregation might think you are singling them out for condemnation, most people gain closeness to you when you look at them. They feel that you are talking to them. The potential for conviction and life-change is enhanced by eye-contact. Also, as they read your face, they participate in the sermon as a conversation. At an airport in Denver I saw a man that I recognized. I caught his eye and nodded my recognition, but there was not time for conversation. Even though I thought we knew each other, as I turned away I realized that I did not know him after all. I had only seen him as the news anchorman for our local news. His eye-contact on screen had created a sense of familiarity that was stirred when I caught his eye in the airport. In a small church when eye-contact takes place there is a knowing between you and the congregant that enriches the sermon.

Some women and men differ on what kinds of gestures they find to be attractive in public speaking. Women like smaller gestures with the hands that stay within the frame of the body. Men like larger gestures that use the full extent of the limbs and involve the whole body. As a rule, women like verbal description and men like sound and action demonstration. These differences should direct you in planning the nonverbal part of delivery to appeal to both genders in various audiences. Also the metaphors, stories, and other illustrative material must meet the audience's specific culture. So consider these in writing the sermon and practicing the sermon.

Other kinds of contacts with the audience have even greater importance in the small church. Invite the audience to look up and read the text for the sermon. This is an invitation to participate in the discovery of God's message and it becomes a binding participation. Occasionally have the whole group read aloud with you. Even though Bible versions vary, the audience hears and verbalizes the text. You can ease the cacophony of various versions being read aloud by supplying the text in a bulletin insert or a slide. Looking up cross references can also be a form of congregation contact. On a few important occasions you can invite the congregation to turn to these references and follow along as you read. On some occasions, have someone prepared to read the portion from the pew or chair. Get the audience to participate by re-reading the text but stop at the key word or words and have the congregation say them aloud. Then make the point of explanation.

You can encourage the small-church audience to respond physically. It can be as simple as asking a rhetorical question that requires a "yes" or "no." Then after pausing and looking at the audience, you affirm aloud the heads that are nodding in agreement. Even with a rhetorical question you could pause for a response and even solicit an answer. You can ask for actions that are common to worship such as bowing the head or raising the hand or you can ask them to remove shoes or take a neighbor's hand. Most small-church audience members will cooperate. You can always ask for an "Amen."

Audience contact takes place outside of worship and the sermon context. When people are leaving after the sermon, it is common for them to compliment the preacher on the sermon. For that, a stock, "thank you" suffices. But for those who add a shared insight or helpful comment it is good to reward those comments with more conversation and encouragement - even the negative ones. This reinforces the interactive contract between you and the congregant. While large churches set up formal focus groups to inform sermon preparation, the small-church community has good opportunities to discuss the sermon through regular interaction. Discussing your sermon preparation and study of the up coming text with a church leader can yield helpful insights. While doing visitation during the week, review your sermon or make a point of the sermon a matter of discussion and prayer. These practices will not only help improve both content and delivery but will also reinforce your contract with the church that is part of the problem-question approach. Each member is supposed to participate in the sermon for the expressed desire of life-change by the grace of God.

Practice

After seminary I took my first field with Village Missions and began to preach using the problem-question format I was trained in. It worked well. The people appreciated my sermons and gave evidence of spiritual growth. However, my main concern in all my efforts was content. I wanted my expositions to be well-researched, well-ordered and theologically accurate. I had been in the ministry more than ten years when, in one of those off hand comments after the sermon, someone provoked me to practice the sermon. I began to practice the sermon on two occasions in the course of preparation for the weekly message. I practiced once at the end of the writing process and again on the morning before the delivering the message. I also recorded the message during each practice and listened to it. I gained my initial goal of greater accuracy and clarity. I also could incorporate into the message more of what the audience needed to respond to. By practicing and listening to a sermon you move to the pew. You hear and respond as the congregation would. If you tell a story where the resolution does not make the point, you can change or drop the story. You can place and time pauses and practice loud histrionic speech or quiet intense speech. You can move in and out of the pulpit to mimic the development of thought. You can include intentional invitations for audience participation, and allow time for a response. Once the sermon has been recorded, it is available for review at any time. Now that I am usually a guest speaker, I take the recording of my sermon with me and listen as I drive or fly to the engagement.

The small church has an aspect of performance that the large congregation does not require. Because the church is small and relationship-based, you must perform the sermon in the context of that relationship. Without practice the sermon becomes an exercise that is disconnected from the continuing relationship you have with the congregation. Practice allows you to accommodate the relationship nature of the sermon in the small church and intentionally invite participation. Practice and listening to the practice helps you eliminate or reduce the space that preaching normally creates between you and the audience and makes the Bible come alive for the audience.

Same Sermon, Different Audience

I walked into a certain preacher's office for the first time. He had been preaching for ten years. On the shelves of his office

I could see the evidence of his history of exposition. Rows of notebooks were neatly lettered with the names of the books of the Bible. As this small-church preacher understood, preaching is not a throwaway enterprise. A sermon is not a product to be used up and disposed. The audience may change, but the content of the sermon does not. Good exposition will adapt, in delivery, to a variety of audiences.

To adapt to a new audience requires some changes. These changes begin with the problem-question. As noted before you may state the problem-question as a different kind of outline (see chapters 9 and 10.) You also may need to adapt the problem-question. This is true if the original problem-question implies a metaphor for the sermon. For example, two sermons that I developed for Luke 1:26 – 38 for different audiences had these two problem-questions, "Like Mary, when does our humility make for our exultation?" and "What are the distinctives of Mary?" If the points answer the question in a diverse and unified way, the different audiences can hear the same material.

The next changes to review are in the conclusion, introduction, and transitions. The sermon's direction for life-change will be different for different audiences. As a result the conclusions for each sermon will be different. In the above sermons on Luke 1:26 – 38 the first one led the congregation to own Mary as a model and imitate her. The second sermon set a pattern for how to react to humbling circumstances. Writing the new conclusion at the end of the body of the sermon made the whole fit for the audience.

You need to change the introduction as well as conclusion. While the contract with the audience in the introduction will remain the same, what is inciteful and insightful will vary (see chapter 11.) In the conclusion you should use what the audience would respond to and connect with in their life circumstances. Every small congregation has stories and there are metaphors that predominate in the culture of any community. You should use these in constructing appropriate introductions and conclusions for different audiences.

Transitions remain the same in that each *wraps up* what has been said in the previous point. Review is both necessary and appropriate with any audience. Transitions also *ramp up* to the next point (see chapter 11) in any sermon for any congregation. However, if the transition is going to *rap up* the point's emotional content, then you must choose the material, story, figure, metaphor, or anecdote to connect with the congregant's life circumstances, knowledge, and experience.

Sermon Notes for Review

The leaders of the boys' program in our small church took the boys out fishing one summer. Fishing had not been going well. It was getting to the hot part of the day and no one had hope for much action. One of the leaders baited two hooks on the same line and said to one of the young boys, "You have to hold your mouth just the right way." He demonstrated a silly half-grin. The boy dropped his line in and dutifully held his mouth in just that position. Soon he felt a tug on the line. When he pulled it in, he had a fish on each hook. When it comes to the nonverbal cues that make for an effective sermon, it is important to "hold your mouth just the right way."

Your attitude must be one of confidence. Without pride or false humility you must see yourself as God's agent to communicate God's message to His people. This attitude will come across in the nonverbal communications of your voice, face, and eyes. In addition to eye-contact you maintain contact with your audience through reading the text and using of cross references. These maintain the invitation to the listeners to participate in the sermon. Contact away from the pulpit also has immense value for you in forming the sermon. Conversing about the sermon with individuals is a source of sermon material as well as a corrective to keep your sermon relevant. Practicing and listening to yourself after practice will greatly enhance all aspects of your delivery as well as allow you to check for accuracy and clarity. At the heart of the sermons you deliver to a small church is a priceless and timeless exposition of Scripture that you can adapt to any church audience.

What three organs must be used in sermon delivery?

1. A heart of confidence.
2. An eye for the people.
3. An ear to hear the sermon as your people would.

SUMMARY

You should both plan and practice certain characteristics for delivery of the sermon to a small-church audience. You must have a clear sense of who you are in relationship to the Lord Jesus Christ and the church. Any part of the written sermon that you direct to the audience is part of rhetorical delivery. This includes the introduction, transitions and conclusion. All of these serve the congregation and provide them direction for participating in the sermon's process. Finally, performance delivery has to do with the nonverbal aspects of delivery such as style and body language.

Appendix

In commemoration of Glenn O'Neal's teaching and influence, here is the text of a sermon that we all heard at some point when we were under his tutelage.[67]

"Prerequisites for a Pulpit Ministry"

Pastor Timothy was having problems. Some of the leaders were challenging his teaching and he was impatient with those who were slow to respond to his exhortations. Not everyone was happy with his ministry. Decisions had to me made. Should he deal with the issues firmly? Should he resign? Should he wait for the problem to resolve itself?

When word of the problem reached the Apostle Paul, he carefully penned a letter "to Timothy, my beloved son..." (II Timothy 1:2).[68] Paul's thoughtful counsel to Timothy has been a source of challenge to Gospel ministers ever since.

Both I and II Timothy have provided a solid basis for establishing standards for young men entering the ministry. The book of II Timothy is especially helpful in providing reassurance to the pastor whose confidence has been shaken by problems similar to those of Timothy. Everyone who is called to proclaim the Word of God must carefully establish principles on which his ministry will be based. Paul warns Timothy that many people will not want teachers who possess such standards when he declares, "...the time will come when they will not endure sound doctrine; but wanting to have Their ears tickled they will accumulate for themselves teachers in accordance to their own desires" (4:3).[69] In other words, some people will look for teachers who say only what they want to hear.

This search may take the form of looking for the preacher with the most abundant supply of jokes or the cleverest use of language. It could involve careful scrutiny of his choice of subject matter, shunning the one who would treat topics which are unpopular. The preacher also may be expected not to preach on anything controversial which, in some situations, would drastically limit his choice of material.

It is sometimes comforting to realize that the dilemma of the preacher is not new. Even in Paul's day there were many by-paths beckoning the one who was attempting to proclaim God's message. Timothy was urged by Paul to "...retain the standard of sound words which you have heard from me..." (1:13a). His reminder to Timothy of these standards should be helpful to every minister in setting his goals for a preaching ministry. They would also prove of benefit to every church as it seeks God's choice for a pulpit minister.

What was the "standard of sound words" to which Paul refers which was a treasure to be guarded (1:14)?

THE MINISTER'S MANNER OF LIFE

The first standard of which he speaks is the *minister's manner of life*. The exhortation to Timothy was, "you therefore, my son, be strong in the grace that is in Christ Jesus" (2:1). A paraphrase of this verse could be, "let every area of your life demonstrate the strength that comes from the grace of the abiding presence of Christ." Before he counseled him as to what he was to say, he dealt with what he was to be. The constancy of complaints from the laity emphasize the fact that the need for this exhortation has not diminished.

One church member put it this way, "If our pastor could fly in on Saturday night, preach on Sunday, and then fly out on Monday morning, everything would be wonderful. He's a good speaker, but when you live in the same community with him and his family through the week, you have difficulty listening to his message on Sunday."

Suffering Hardship

An important area of strength relating to the minister's manner of life is the *willingness to "suffer hardship"* for the honor of Jesus Christ. Paul invited him to "suffer hardship with me" (2:3) or, in other words, "take your share of the suffering."

This is in contrast to statements commonly heard among ministers and prospective ministers: "He really has an ideal setup in that church," or, "I'm glad to hear he received the advancement. He deserved a call to a larger church."

Three illustrations emphasize the task of the ministry and all speak of the personal sacrifice involved. The soldier only succeeds as he suffers hardship in pleasing the one who enlisted him (2:3, 4). The athlete receives the prize by following the rules laid down by others (2:5). The farmer receives his share of the crops only after working hard (2:6). Paul concludes this exhortation by presenting what should be a continuous challenge to those who would use the ministry for their own purposes: he was willing to "suffer hardship, even imprisonment as a criminal" (2:9), for the honor of the Christ he served.

Personal Purity

Another necessary characteristic of the minister's manner of life is a *demonstration of personal purity*. The last statement of 2:19 is, "...Let every one who names the name of the Lord abstain from wickedness." Paul then compares the servant of the Lord to the pot or pan used in a home and declares that "if a man cleanses himself from these things, he will by a vessel for honor, sanctified, useful to the Master, prepared for every good work" (2:21). The "these things" evidently refers to the aforementioned wickedness which was being perpetrated by the worldly and empty chatter of Hymenaeus and Philetus. Paul stresses the diligence with which one must seek this inner purity and flee from youthful lusts, and pursue after righteousness, faith, love and peace, with those who call on the Lord from a pure heart" (2:22).

The message which the preacher delivers begins long before he enters the pulpit. It starts in the demonstration of words and deeds which his audience has observed. It may come from a good reputation which has been reported by others. However it comes, there is no justification for a minister to expect a favorable response to his message, or to assume his congregation will build a sincere purpose of life, unless he himself has responded whole heartedly in the dedication of his life to Christ.

THE MINISTER'S ATTITUDE TOWARD PEOPLE

The second "standard of sound words" of which Paul speaks, involves *the minster's attitude toward people.*

A rude awakening for many ministers is the slow response of people to the simple gospel of Jesus Christ, and their hesitancy to grow in the Christian life.

Constantly the minister is faced with discouragements as he attempts to minister to the needs of his flock. Slight differences in minor points of doctrine become the test of whether one Christian will fellowship with another. A divergence of views on some organizational policy sows seeds of division which seem never to be healed.

Timothy was experiencing a conflict over the teaching of a divisive doctrine. There were those who had been spreading the idea "...that the resurrection has already taken place, and thus they upset the faith of some (2:18).

The reaction of a pastor to such problems usually takes one of two forms. The easiest way out is to become discouraged and quit. "I love to preach," he might reason, "but I just can't stand these unstable people!" Another possible response is to exert his authority with severity. "I'm going to clean up this problem if it's the last thing I do." "What this church needs is a good house cleaning!" The trouble with the latter response is that often when the broom has swept clean, he has no one left to listen to him preach, or pay his salary!

Loving As Christ Loves

Paul reminds Timothy that a part of being "strong in the grace that is in Christ Jesus" (2:1) is to demonstrate to people the same love that caused Christ to pray for those who were crucifying him: "Father, forgive them for they do not know what they are doing" (Luke 23:34). Paul's word to Timothy was, "The Lord's bondservant must not be quarrelsome, but be kind to all, able to teach, patient when wronged, with gentleness correcting those who are in opposition..." (2:24, 25a). The pastor constantly encounters those who vex his soul because of their selfish opposition to the advancement of the cause of Christ. Not all of these will be outside the church of Christ. The effective minister must develop the attitude of forbearance by constantly reminding himself that every individual is a soul for whom Christ died and thus has value and exciting potential.

Paul left no delusions as to the task before him in dealing with wicked men ensnared by the devil (2:26). He even suggested that "in the last days" these men will be even more intense in their opposition (3:1). Some of the attributes listed were, "...lovers of self, lovers of money, boastful, arrogant, revilers, disobedient to parents, ungrateful, unholy, unloving, irreconcilable, malicious gossips, without self-control, brutal, haters of good, treacherous, reckless, conceited, lovers of pleasure rather than lovers of God" (3:2-4).

In spite of these discouraging prospects, Paul concludes his exhortation to Timothy by declaring that "I solemnly charge you in the presence of God and of Christ Jesus, who is to judge the living and the dead, ...preach the Word..." (4:1, 2a).

In determining his attitude toward people, the effective preacher should keep constantly in mind that everyone with whom he speaks, no matter how unresponsive, will have to answer to Jesus Christ. This is a sobering thought, and the basis for challenge. The minster is to "...be ready in season and out of season; reprove, rebuke, exhort, with great patience and instruction" (4:2).

In spite of the fact that one must look at opposition from the world realistically, a constant encouragement to the minister is the possibility that "God may grant them repentance leading to the knowledge of the truth, and they may come to their senses and escape from the snare of the devil..." (2:25, 26). One of the greatest joys that comes to a pastor is to see lives who have been "delivered...from the domain of darkness, and transferred... to the kingdom of His beloved Son" (Colossians 1:13). If ever the preacher loses the expectation of the transformation of lives, he has lost much of his effectiveness.

In spite of the deceivers there are many who come to the Lord, grow in the faith and constantly demonstrate the reality of the power of God in their lives. These are the ones of whom Paul speaks as he tells Timothy that "...the things which you have heard from me in the presence of many witnesses, these entrust to faithful men, who will be able to teach others also" (2:2). To see one's ministry multiplied by the teaching program of those who have responded to the gospel because of his efforts, that is the reward which spurs the pastor to constantly minister to a world that is being "...held captive..." (2:26).

After serving as a pastor for twenty-five years, it has been my observation that the people who produce joy in the ministry are legion. Even though the foregoing warning in regard to the wicked and deceitful is legitimate, the rewards of observing the responsive causes the miseries produced by those who would oppose the work of Christ to fade into insignificance.

THE MINISTER'S PRESENTATION OF THE WORD OF GOD

A further "standard of sound words" worthy of consideration is *instruction in relation to the presentation of the Word of God.*

Evidently Timothy was in danger of succumbing to the temptation of minimizing the importance of the forthright proclamation of the Word of God. Perhaps the opposition had caused him to reduce his forcefulness, or the false teachers had lured him in the snare of dealing with side issues. Whatever the problem, Paul exhorted him "...to kindle afresh the gift of God which is in you through the laying on of my hands. For God has not given us a spirit of timidity, but of power and love and discipline. Therefore, do not be ashamed of the testimony of our Lord, or of me His prisoner; but join with me in suffering for the gospel according to the power of God" (1:6-8).

Through out the book Paul constantly challenges Timothy to present God's message with confidence and enthusiasm. Of particular help are his answers to four questions that are vital for an effective ministry of the Word of God.

1. Why should one believe it?

He first of all points out that the basis for boldness in preaching the gospel is the fact that God's eternal plan has been made sure by "...the appearing of our Savior Christ Jesus, who abolished death, and brought life and immortality to light through the gospel" (1:10). The appearance of Christ after his death is a substantiation for the claims about Christ recorded in the Old Testament. He chided the doubting disciples by declaring, "O foolish men and slow of heart to believe in all that the prophets have spoken!" (Luke 24:25). Luke then affirms that "...beginning with Moses and with all the prophets, He explained to them the things concerning Himself in all the Scriptures" (Luke 24:27). Thus the risen Christ places His stamp of approval upon the authority of the Old Testament.

The Bible is constantly under attack. The one who is called to preach the Word of God must be convinced that God has spoken! Paul gives the reassuring affirmation that "all Scripture is inspired by God..." (3:16). The preacher's task is to proclaim that revelation.

2. What is the central theme of God's revelation?

The thrust of the apostle's message found in his challenge to "remember Jesus Christ, risen from the dead, descendant of David, according to my gospel" (2:8). Proper occupation with these truths which involve the person of Christ, the purpose of His first coming, and the promise of the second coming, will be a constant deterrent to wrangling about words without purpose (2:14), and engaging in "...worldly and empty chatter..." (2:16).

It is apparent that the whole Word of God focuses upon this major theme as it is found in the entire Word of God. Paul counsels Timothy to "Be diligent to present yourself approved unto God as a workman who does not need to be ashamed, handling accurately the word of truth" (2:15). The "workman" with which he would be most familiar would be the tent maker. It is interesting to note the word "handling accurately" literally means "to cut straight." Now what would cause a tentmaker to be most embarrassed? Probably it would be to have a piece of material fail to fit the pattern because he had not cut it straight. His plea is obvious. Be careful in the treatment of the Word so that all the pieces fit together according to God's plan.

3. What will the effect be on the hearer?

The first effect will be enlightenment which will lead the hearer to a knowledge of Christ as his Savior. Paul reminds Timothy "...that from childhood you have known the sacred writings which are able to give you the wisdom that leads to salvation through faith which is in Christ Jesus" (3:15).

Once a person has responded to the gospel, the Word of God becomes the means by which he is equipped for a productive Christian life (3:17). It is good for "teaching" (3:16) because it is the infallible source of truth. "Reproof" (3:16) probably refers to that which enables one to refute the false teacher but could also involve the ability to resist any suggestion which would lead to looseness of morals. "Correction" (3:16) refers to improvements or revisions of life necessary to put a person on the path of pleasing God. "Training in righteousness" (3:16) enables one to mature in his dedication to Christ with a growing discernment of His will in every phase of life.

4. How should one proclaim the Word?

The command is to "preach the Word ..." (4:2). The usual word emphasis given to this phrase is "Preach the *Word.*" However, there are reasons to believe that the intent was for the word stress to be "*Preach* the Word." This is indicated by the solemnity of the charge given in verse one, and the meaning of the word "preach" which is "to herald a message." Further evidence for this contention is emphasized by the words "be ready in season and out of season" (4:2) which would seemingly refer to the action of preaching.

Most people would agree that there is a dire need for preachers who herald the message with urgency. There are many sincere, dedicated ministers of the gospel, but it is alarming to find that many of them sound like they don't really believe the message they preach. In contrast to the ability of a great actor to make that which is unreal become real, many preachers make what is real seem very unreal. One remedy is for the minister daily to ask the Lord to make the message of God's revelation vitally important; ask Him for a sense of urgency stemming from the high privilege of and responsibility he has in proclaiming it; and ask him for enablement from the Holy Spirit to proclaim the message with life-saving power.

Not only must this message be presented with urgency, but it needs to be proclaimed vividly. Paul didn't say this in his letter to Timothy, but he practiced it. He constantly used enlightening illustrations which made the truth come to life.

Notice several vivid illustrations in chapter two, some of which have already been mentioned. He used three pictures to stress the idea of dedication to the task; the soldier (3, 4), the athlete (5), and the farmer (6). He compared the diligence of one who handles the Word of God to a workman who does not want to be embarrassed with his work (15). The word of wicked Hymenaeus and Philetus is referred to as "gangrene" (17). The analogy is made between the honored servant and the honored vessel in a large house (20, 21). He concluded with a reference to the state of the deceived as being "held captive" in "the snare of the devil" (26).

If a preacher would apply himself diligently to the task of developing applicable illustrations, he would find a marked improvement in the attention of the listeners as well as their comprehension of the message. The Lord apparently felt this was a necessity. He constantly spoke of the sower who went to sow, the prodigal son, the ones on whom the tower of Siloam fell, the wedding feast. He presented spiritual truth by employing illustrations from the everyday activities of people. Preachers would do well to take some lessons in this regard from the Master Teacher!

So far we have talked about three standards that are of vital concern to the minister; namely, his manner of life, his attitude toward people, and his presentation of the Word of God. The Lord we serve, the life-giving message we have to proclaim, and the eternal welfare of the souls for whom we are responsible demand that we not be satisfied with mediocrity. The ministry must be challenged to higher standards.

Again Paul's words to Timothy were, "Retain the standard of sound words which you have heard from me, in the faith and love which are in Christ Jesus. Guard through the Holy Spirit who dwells in us, the treasure which has been entrusted to you" (1:13, 14).

(Endnotes)

1   Carl S. Dudley, <u>Effective Small Churches in the Twenty-first Century</u> (Nashville: Abingdon, 2003), 11.

2   Dudley, 12.

3   Lyle E. Schaller, <u>The Small Church is Different</u> (Nashville: Abingdon, 1982), 41.

4   Glenn Daman, <u>Shepherding the Small Church: A Leadership Guide for the Majority of Today's Churches</u> (Grand Rapids: Kregel, 2002), 42-51.

5   Malcolm Gladwell, <u>The Tipping Point: How Little Things Can Make a Big Difference</u> (New York: Little and Brown, 2000), 197.

6   Daman, 57.

7   John A. Broadus, <u>On the Preparation and Delivery of Sermons, ed. Jesse B. Weatherspoon</u> (New York: Harper and Row 1944), 3.

8   Haddon W. Robinson, <u>Biblical Preaching</u> (Grand Rapids: Baker, 2001), 21.

9   Glenn O'Neal, <u>Make the Bible Live: A Basic Guide for Preachers and Teachers</u> (Winona Lake: BMH, 1979), 27

10 Dr. Lori Carrell, <u>The Great American Sermon Survey</u> (Wheaton: Mainstay Church Resources, 2000), 114.

11 O'Neal, 27.

12 Vernal R. Wilkinson, Jr. <u>Exposition in Small and Rural Churches</u> (Dissertation for Faith Seminary, 2007), 51.

13 Timothy George, "Doctrinal Preaching", in <u>Handbook of Contemporary</u>

Preaching, ed. Michael Duduit (Nashville: Broadman & Holman, 1992), 96.

14 Calvin Miller, "Narrative Preaching", in Handbook of Contemporary Preaching. ed. Michael Duduit (Nashville: Broadman & Holman, 1992), 103

15 David Ray, Wonderful Worship in Smaller Churches (Cleveland: Pilgrim Press, 2000), 106.

16 Laurence A. Wagley, Preaching with the Small Congregation (Nashville: Abingdon, 1989), 48ff.

17 Daman, 81, 83.

18 Leon Hill, O for the Life of a Preacher (Amarillo: Baxter Lane, 1975), 19.

19 Leon Hill, O' For the Life of a Preacher (Amarillo: Baxter Lane, 1975), 12.

20 Steve R. Bierly, How to Thrive as a Small-Church Pastor (Grand Rapids: Zondervan, 1998), 45.

21 Glenn O'Neal, Make the Bible Live: A Basic Guide for Preachers and Teachers (Winona Lake: BMH, 1979), 51.

22 Ibid.

23 Ibid.

24 O'Neal, 53.

25 O'Neal, 51.

26 O'Neal, 52.

27 Archibald Thomas Robertson, Word Pictures in the New Testament, 6vols. (Nashville, Broadman, 1930) 34.

28 Robertson, 2:34.

29 Ben Witherington III, Conflict & Community in Corinth: a Socio-Rhetorical Commentary on 1 and 2 Corinthians (Grand Rapids: Eerdmans, 1995), 40.

30 O'Neal, 51.

31 H. Wayne House and Daniel G. Garland, God's Message, Your Sermon: Discover, Develop, and Deliver What God Meant by What He Said (Nashville: Thomas Nelson, 2007), 58.

32 O'Neal, 51.

33 House and Garland, 65.

34 House and Garland, 69.

35 House and Garland, 63.

36 Haddon W. Robinson, Biblical Preaching: The Development and Delivery of Expository Messages (Grand Rapids: Baker, 2001), 21, 33.

37 Lori Carrell, The Great American Sermon Survey (Wheaton: Mainstay, 2000), 117.

38 Carrell, 115.

39 Alex Montoya, <u>Preaching with Passion</u> (Grand Rapids: Kregel, 2000), 12.

40 John MacArthur, Jr. <u>Rediscovering Expository Preaching</u>, ed. Richard Mahue (Nashville: Word, 1992), 11.

41 Robertson McQuilken, "Spiritual Formation Through Preaching: Four components of preaching that changes lives" in <u>The Art and Craft of Biblical Preaching</u>. ed. Haddon Robinson and Craig Brian Larson (Grand Rapids: Zondervan, 2005), 48.

42 William H. Willimon & Robert Wilson, <u>Preaching and Worship in the Small Church</u> (Nashville: Abingdon, 1980), 107.

43 Glenn O'Neal, <u>Make the Bible Live: A Basic Guide for Preachers and Teachers</u> (Winona Lake: BMH Books, 1979), 6.

44 O'Neal, 32.

45 Ibid

46 R. Albert Mohler, Jr. <u>He is not Silent: Preaching in a Postmodern World</u> (Chicago: Moody Publishers, 2008), 16 – 20.

47 O'Neal, 32 – 33.

48 Carl Dudley, <u>Making the Small Church Effective</u> (Nashville: Abingdon, 1979), 56 – 57.

49 Arlin J. Rothauge, <u>Sizing Up a Congregation for New Member Ministry</u> (New York: Episcopal Church Center, na), 7 – 8.

50 Charles Caldwell Ryrie, <u>The Ryrie Study Bible</u> (Chicago: Moody, 1978), 1052.

51 Bryan Chapell, <u>Christ-centered Preaching: redeeming the expository sermon</u> (Grand Rapids: Baker, 2005), 48 – 52.

52 Donald R. Sunukjian, <u>Invitation to Biblical Preaching: Proclaiming Truth with Clarity and Relevance</u> (Grand Rapids: Kregel, 2007), 51.

53 O'Neal, 33 – 34.

54 Of the following outlines some are from O'Neal, 81 – 110 or from the author's sermons.

55 Leon Hill, O, <u>For the Life of a Preacher</u> (Amarillo: Baxter Lane, 1975), 41

56 Leon Hill, O, <u>For the Life of a Preacher</u> (Amarillo: Baxter Lane, 1975), 18.

57 D. Martyn Lloyd-Jones, <u>Preaching and Preachers</u> (Grand Rapids: Zondervan, 1971), 85.

58 Glenn O'Neal, <u>Make the Bible Live: A Basic Guide for Preachers and Teachers</u> (Winona Lake: BMH Books, 1979), 38.

59 O'Neal, 121.

60 John Broadus, <u>On the Preparation and Delivery of Sermons</u>, ed. Jesse B. Weatherspoon (New York: Harper & Row, 1944), 326.

61 O'Neal, 64.

62 Leland Ryken, James C. Wilhoit and Tremper Longman III, ed. <u>Dictionary of Biblical Imagery</u> (Downers Grove: IVP), 1998.

63 Larry Smith, "Really Short Stories" <u>AARP The Magazine</u>, July & August 2009, 8.

64 Hill, 18.

65 Hill, 52.

66 Ibid.

67 Glenn F. O'Neal, <u>Make the Bible Live: A Basic guide for Preachers and Teachers</u> (Winona Lake: BMH Books, 1979), 13ff.

68 All quotations are taken from the New American Standard Version, 1977.

69 All verse references in this sermon are from II Timothy unless otherwise noted.

CPSIA information can be obtained
at www.ICGtesting.com
Printed in the USA
BVHW071508251118
533935BV00001B/212/P